YOU
CAN HAVE A
NEAR-PERFECT
MEMORY

YOU
CAN HAVE A
NEAR-PERFECT
MEMORY

Mort Herold

Contemporary Books, Inc.
Chicago

Library of Congress Cataloging in Publication Data

Herold, Mort.
    You can have a near-perfect memory.

    1. Mnemonics.   I. Title.
BF385.H44   153.1'4   81-69601
ISBN 0-8092-5943-5   AACR2

Published by Contemporary Books, Inc.
180 North Michigan Avenue, Chicago, Illinois 60601
Manufactured in the United States of America
Library of Congress Catalog Card Number: 81-69601
International Standard Book Number: 0-8092-5943-5

Published simultaneously in Canada by
Beaverbooks, Ltd.
150 Lesmill Road
Don Mills, Ontario M3B 2T5
Canada

To Cressida, June, and Richard
with love and gratitude for your
encouragement, help, and patience.

And in memory of my father.

Memory performs the impossible for man; holds together past and present, gives continuity and dignity to human life. This is the companion, this the tutor, the poet, the library, with which you travel.

Mark Van Doren
Liberal Education

Contents

YOU
CAN HAVE A
NEAR-PERFECT
MEMORY

Part I:
Introduction to
Memory Control

My mind is like a tape recorder with one button—erase.

Andy Warhol

1

The Three R's of Remembering

Inside your head is the most miraculous and complex remembering device on Earth. Despite this fact, few people ever use as much as 1 percent of their actual memory capacity, and they waste the other 99 percent by violating the natural laws of memory.

Whether you believe it or not, at this very moment you have enough natural memory capability to duplicate any of the most remarkable memory feats you have ever witnessed—a faultless recollection of intricate and extensive technical information or the perfect recall of the names and faces of a hundred people met for the first time. You *can* do this—and more.

But can this be done by "improving your memory"? Sorry, the answer is no. Your memory itself is not a "thing" that needs to be improved, as though it were an appliance in need of repair. Barring brain damage or severe psychological problems, there is nothing wrong with your present memory. It is perfect as it is. Unlike a "thing," your memory is a continuous information processing system, which, when understood, will enable you to exert your own direction and control, resulting in the kind of memory performance you never thought possible.

The secret of maximum memory performance is not in your

memory itself, but in how you *use* it. The term *memory improvement* is an overworked misnomer. The answer is not to improve your memory, but to control it! When you have trouble remembering something it is not because of the brain you were born with, but simply because you are not using a memory technique that will make it easier for your brain to remember. What you remember (or forget) depends on what you *do* to assure later recall, rather than on whether or not you "have" a good memory. In short, you do not need a better memory. You just need to know how to remember better.

YOU CAN HAVE A NEAR-PERFECT MEMORY presents new concepts that enable you to reduce dramatically your present forgetting and to commit things to memory without old-fashioned, tiresome repetition. In effect, you will remember *without* memorizing.

It is important to realize that your memory is a continuous information processing system. It consists of three stages, which are called the *Three Rs of Memory*:

1. **Registration:** Learning the material in the first place.
2. **Retention:** Storage of the information until needed.
3. **Retrieval:** Getting the information back out.

   □ When your mind processes information effectively in all three stages, such information can be successfully remembered.
   □ A failure in *any one* of these three stages will result in a failure of memory performance.

When all is said and done, you will either remember something or forget it—depending on how effectively your mind processes that information. *Control the process, and you control the memory.*

The odds are overwhelming that you were never taught the techniques of Memory Control as part of your regular schooling. Such information was either not known or not part of the curriculum. You probably remember your teachers saying, "This material must be learned by tomorrow. Now go home and memorize it." But they did not tell you *how* to memorize it, and that was that! Whatever memory anxiety you still experience was born during your early schooling. You learned what to know, but not how to remember it.

Still, very few people today have developed control over their day-to-day learning and remembering. Most people are not even aware of the existence of Memory Control as a learnable skill. With casual, undirected, hit-or-miss habits of recall, most people have about as much control over their memory as non-drivers have at the wheel of a car. The sad truth is that most people still live their whole lives this way. And as a result they inevitably develop the gnawing suspicion (or belief) that what they have is a "poor memory."

> *There are no poor memories.*
> *There are only untrained memories.*

What you have is not a poor memory, but an untrained memory. If it is unreliable, it is *because* it is untrained. The fact that you have eyes wasn't enough to make you an instant reader. You first had to learn the alphabet, the letter sounds, and then words, phrases, and sentences. You followed a plan that eventually produced results, and now you are able to read with much enjoyment, much profit, and little effort.

Similarly, you can't necessarily remember everything you want to remember, just because you have "a memory." As reading is a worthwhile skill, so is the skill of memory. You have trained your eyes to read, and you can train your brain to remember.

GETTING THE MOST FROM THIS BOOK

This is not an instant memory course; there are no gimmicks. All the methods are based on sound psychological principles and the established laws of learning and memory. Like any worthwhile skill, good remembering takes both know-how and effort. But the methods themselves are surprisingly easy to learn and enjoyable to use. They work. All that is required is for you to work them. Virtually all the techniques you will learn will work right away; they are therefore immediately useful.

Common sense tells us that the purpose of a good memory is simply to remember what needs to be remembered. The purpose of this book is to give you the tools of Memory Control so that you can indeed remember what you need and want to remember, for as long as you choose to remember it.

My instructions are clear, simple, and direct; but please remember that merely reading this book is not enough. Get your full money's worth by actively participating as directed and by using the ideas and procedures I will be teaching. When you do this, substantial results must inevitably follow. You don't need to feel that you have a "poor memory" any more than a dull knife must remain in that condition. You sharpen it!

It is time for you to realize what a magnificent memory mechanism lies between your ears. It is a sleeping giant, and it is time for you to awaken it.

2

Awakening Your
Sleeping Giant:
The Brain Chain

If I were to ask you at this moment if you could look at a list of a dozen unrelated items and then, without looking, repeat them back in correct order, how would you respond? I suspect that your answer would be similar to that of thousands of other people: "You can't be serious. I don't have that kind of memory."

But you do have that kind of memory; what's more, you have it right now. I won't ask you to take my word for this. I would rather let you prove it to yourself as you learn the Brain Chain technique.

I call it the Brain Chain because it involves mentally linking things together to form a complete chain. It's a simple exercise in imagination. All you have to do is mentally picture various objects in the way that I ask you to picture them. Here's the list we're going to use—a dozen different, unrelated items taken at random. For the moment, just glance at them briefly and then read on.

Wristwatch
Sausage
Dog
Apple
Violin
Butter
Rolls Royce
Chimpanzee
Baseball bat
Airplane
Swimming pool
Coffee.

All right, now we're ready. Don't write anything down. Just read and relax, but follow the simple directions *exactly*, even if they seem a bit unusual. Remember that this is an exercise in imagination, and your job is to picture vividly each of the list items in the way that I suggest until we've done them all.

Incidentally, don't try to visualize the words as groups of letters. For example, for wristwatch, visualize not the words but a watch! It's very important to see the action, as I describe it, as clearly and vividly as you can in your mind's eye. Just let go and enjoy the pictures we make together as we go along. You'll be picturing some strange or unusual interaction between the items, which will hold them together link by link, until the Brain Chain is complete. Just follow the simple directions very closely.

The first item is a WRISTWATCH. Right now, in your mind's eye, picture that watch, as clearly as you can, on your wrist. Just a moment or two is long enough. It's not how long you see the object that counts, but the *quality* of your mental imagery. It's not necessary to close your eyes to picture it mentally, but if it helps, do so. Make it as easy as you can, but see that watch *now*, on your wrist. Now see it suddenly unbuckle itself, jump into the air, and strap itself around a long, smelly, red SAUSAGE, which is floating by in the air. See it now! (Yes, I know it seems strange and illogical, but this is one of the reasons it works, as you'll see.) Now is the time to see the wristwatch tightly squeezing that red sausage. That *smelly* sausage. Smell it if you can. The more senses that come into play, the better, as far as your memory is concerned.

Here we are with the wristwatch strapped tightly around the sausage. Now, mentally zoom in close to that sausage and see it floating in the air toward a big, hungry, barking DOG. This dog *loves* sausage, so see him lunge for it and chew it up with great gusto. No more sausage. Only the dog.

The next item on our list is APPLE. Picture an incredibly large green apple sitting on the dog's back. It is the biggest green apple you ever saw. It must be a foot wide! Zoom in and see it clearly—now. If you look closely, you can see a crack forming, and it suddenly splits the apple wide open, revealing a VIOLIN inside, playing all by itself. See and hear the violin playing.

The next item is BUTTER. So now link violin and butter. Just see the violin fall out of the apple, land on a tremendous mound of yellow butter, and slowly sink into that butter, disappearing completely. Now all you can see is that big mound of yellow butter. But look closely! See it as it begins to grow bigger, and bigger, and gradually takes on the unmistakable shape of an automobile—a ROLLS ROYCE! See it clearly—a yellow Rolls Royce made of butter! Every part of the body is yellow except the windows, which you can see through. Now look into the driver's window and see a CHIMPANZEE in the driver's seat. See him now, with a toothy grin, as he waves at you. Suddenly he jumps out of the car, picks up a BASEBALL BAT, and throws it high into the air. Follow the baseball bat. It goes so high that it collides with an orange AIRPLANE. See the action! The orange plane is hit so hard that it has to land. Now see that airplane starting to come down slowly and landing gently in a blue SWIMMING POOL with beautiful clear blue water. See it now. But look at what is happening to that cool blue water: It's turning coffee-brown and starts to steam like fresh coffee. It has, indeed, turned into COFFEE. A pool full of it! So try to inhale the aroma of that fresh pool of coffee.

All right, that takes care of the twelve items. Since this is your first exposure to this Brain Chain technique, here is a quick review. Be sure to see the action as you read and mentally review the following picture story.

Your WRISTWATCH unbuckles itself, jumps into the air, and straps itself around a smelly, red

SAUSAGE. The sausage floats in the air, over to a hungry, barking

DOG. The dog chews up the juicy sausage. On the dog's back is an incredibly large green

APPLE, which is a foot wide and splits open to reveal a

VIOLIN, which is playing sweetly all by itself. But the violin falls out of the apple, landing on and sinking into a tremendous mound of yellow

BUTTER. The mound of yellow butter expands visibly into the size and shape of a bright yellow

ROLLS ROYCE! And sitting in the driver's seat is a

CHIMPANZEE. The chimp waves at you, jumps out, and picks up a

BASEBALL BAT, which he throws way up into the sky, hitting a passing orange

AIRPLANE, which is now damaged from the impact and begins to come down and gently land in a clear blue

SWIMMING POOL. The clear cool water suddenly becomes steaming hot and dark brown as it turns into a pool full of

COFFEE!

That's it. Now, take your pencil and paper and try to recall and write down each of the twelve items, in order, starting with the first one, which was on your wrist. Before you try this, here is a tip on *how* to do it: All you have to do is simply picture each item and its action in the story. Each one will bring the next item back to you, one after the other, until you have recreated exactly the same scenario you just visualized.

Now put the book down, take a pencil and paper, and write down the list before you read on. When you finish, check your list against the one in the book.

Well, how did it go? In all probability you did very well and found it surprisingly easy to retrieve just about all of the twelve items in the correct order. If you were actively participating when we made the original mental pictures, you should have had no trouble reproducing all or almost all the items on the list. If you missed more than two, go back to the place where the original instructions are given for each picture and actively participate once more. Then score yourself again. You'll be delighted.

Make note of a very important fact: I *never* told you to "memorize" anything, just to *picture it*! In effect, you have committed to memory a dozen items, in order, without "memorizing" them through tiresome repetition.

The purpose of this exercise was to give you an illustration of your own natural memory power and how it can be released with simple techniques of associative picturing. Although the control techniques you'll be using later on are more sophisticated, the idea of remembering without memorizing is central to the book. The technique you have just experienced is basic in memory training. We purposely used bizarre interaction with these pictures. Either plausible or bizarre picturing can be used, and they will be, as we go along. The choice will be made on the basis of what works best for you. In this exercise I've told you specifically what to picture, just to get you started. As we progress you will learn how to do your own picturing and associating in the way that is most natural and vivid for you. The pictures *you* decide to use will work far better for your memory than any that I might suggest.

Mental picturing and association are two of the mind's most basic powers, and they are continually active, whether or not you are aware of them. Because of these powers, you are able to learn, remember, think, read, and speak. But when you are able to direct these two forces (among others) you can then make your memory work *for* you and not against you. And not just with irrelevant and simple word lists, but for entirely practical purposes. You'll be able to remember names, facts, numbers, practical lists of daily things to do, and information of all other types. You will actually be controlling the input and output of your memory as you did a moment ago with that list of twelve items.

This twelve-word Brain Chain should make you aware that memory performance is not only a learnable skill, but one that responds beautifully and *quickly* to training.

All of the methods and techniques that follow are based on the established laws of learning and remembering. We will be capitalizing on them by putting them into practical use through the use of basic learning skills and strategies and mnemonic techniques. Like all worthwhile skills, improving your memory's performance will take practice. Based on what you've just accomplished with the Brain Chain, I think you will agree that the results will be worth the effort.

Now for something that may surprise you: I said at the beginning of this chapter that your present memory is capable of remembering a list of a dozen unrelated words. But suppose I say that your memory is also keen enough to recall that entire list *backward.*

Before you proceed, try this. You don't need a pencil and paper. Just recall the words as they come to you. *All you have to do is start with the last word, COFFEE, and think in reverse—just mentally review each of the pictures, as before, but going backward.* Each item will bring the preceding item to mind, all the way back to the first item. It works just as easily, forward or backward! *Start slowly,* and you'll pick up speed as you go along. Now, put the book down and recall those twelve words in reverse order.

When you have finished successfully, you may congratulate yourself. You have begun to awaken your sleeping giant.

3

The Control of Your Magnificent Memory Machine

During recent years, memory researchers have come up with much valuable information that is beginning to clear up some of the age-old memory mysteries. The most practical way to understand your memory better is to take an active part in the simple exercises that follow.

I am going to ask you to do something, which will take only a moment. Here it is: *Remember!* Do this now, before going on.

Unless I am mistaken, you are not sure what I mean by that direction. You are wondering exactly *what* I want you to remember. It is doubtful that my sudden instruction to you to "remember" produced any particular response, image, or association from your past experience. This is, of course, because I did not give you any cue as to *what* to remember. *In order to function, your memory needs and must have a cue to activate the retrieval process.*

Now let's try that again, this time a bit differently. Please respond as quickly as you can to this revised instruction: *Remember your street address.*

Good. If I were to ask you the question *"When did he discover it?"* your response would no doubt be "Who?" or "What?" You'd be asking for exactly what your mind needs and must have—some specific cue—to search your memory for a particular fact, figure, or other item of information. When a cue is added to the question—*"When did Columbus discover America?"*—it is much easier for your mind to produce the correct answer.

Now, one more question. Take a moment or two to answer, if necessary. *"What did you have for breakfast this morning?"* Answer before going on.

It goes without saying that you were able to answer these questions easily and quickly, even though the last one may have taken a moment longer. What you actually did in each case was to search your memory, find the right information, and deliver it. But the point is that what *enabled* you to search for the specific answer or information, locate it, and retrieve it was the specific *retrieval cue* given in each question. When I asked you to remember your street address, the words *your street address* formed the retrieval cue that immediately activated the delivery of your answer—and all in less time than it took to blink your eye. When I asked, "When did Columbus discover America?" the answer "1492" instantly popped into your mind.

The basic memory unit in Memory Control training is the retrieval cue. Why do retrieval cues work? They work because these cues themselves are closely related, associated, or connected with the exact information they retrieve. The words *your street address* form a retrieval cue that immediately retrieves that with which it is associated—your particular house number and street, as well as your city, state, country, continent, hemisphere, planet, solar system, galaxy, and universe. You can follow the associative pathway as far as you like! Any or all of these things can spring to mind quickly and naturally, through simple *association*, when triggered by a retrieval cue.

Please answer this question now: *"What is your birthdate?"* This question is a powerful cue that has an ingrained association with a particular month, date, and year, which no doubt automatically popped into your conscious mind (from your subconscious memory bank) through the immediate action of association. Again, when I asked, *"What did you have for breakfast this morning?"* this specific cue cut off all other lines of recall except those that led to bacon, eggs, and coffee or whatever foods you associate with breakfast. *Such association is involved in all of our thinking and remembering.* Whatever thought or fact springs to mind, you can be sure that it was triggered by some kind of cue, either from within or from without. *One thing brings to mind another.* This is the universal Reminder Principle at work. This is so basic that we take it for granted and are hardly aware of it. Most of Memory Control training is centered around the operation of such cues (or reminders) and the responses they elicit. "All you need is a reminder" is a basic tenet in memory training.

Each cue and its response constitutes the action and reaction of association. When something you see or hear (or smell, touch, or taste) reminds you of something, whatever *reminded you* is the retrieval cue, and what it *reminds you of* is the response. Basically, this is the way your memory works.

There is no computer on Earth now, nor in the forseeable future, that can do this instant and automatic associating *except your own brain, your mind, your memory.*

In 1890 the brilliant Harvard psychologist William James stated some timeless truths about memory. He said that the human mind is, essentially, an *associating machine.* He also said:

> ...The more other facts a fact is associated with in the mind, the better possession of it our mind retains. Each of its associates becomes a hook to which it hangs, a means to fish it up by when sunk beneath the surface. *The "secret of a good memory" is thus the secret of forming diverse and multiple associations with every fact we care to retain.*

*William James, *Principles of Psychology*, Vol. 1 (New York: Henry Holt & Co., 1890), p. 662.

Put in a different way, the more retrieval cues you associate with a fact you want to retain, the easier the *recall* will be later on when you use any or all of those original retrieval cues to "fish up" the desired information. The reason for this is that the more associations you make, the more *meaning* there is for your mind to work with, and, therefore, the easier and quicker the retrieval.

It is important to remember that James's principle of "diverse and multiple associations" is a basic principle upon which this book's concept of Memory Control is based.

The following is an interesting practical example of the power of association in action. I'm going to give you single cue words (retrieval cues), and I want you to respond with the first word that pops into your mind. For example, if the cue is HAM, you might respond with EGGS or any other word that cue brings to mind. If the cue is JOKE, it might retrieve from your memory LAUGH, COMEDIAN, or any of many other associations your mind has made during your lifetime of experience. There are no "right" or "wrong" responses. They are all valid. Whatever you are reminded of by the cue is your response.

Here are the cues. Please respond to each of them, one at a time:

1. SUNDAY
2. BASKET
3. HOLIDAY
4. DOCTOR
5. LOVE
6. STOMACH

Please notice that your responses were probably made quickly and with little if any thinking. The reason? Each of the above cue words, which could have been *any* words, *was already associated with something else in your mind.* That other thing just popped to the surface when retrieved by the cue. If a hundred people attend one of my memory seminars, I might get a hundred different responses to each cue. Since everyone's experience is different, many different responses are to be expected.

Memory is defined as our ability to retain and revive past impressions. All your knowledge and experience is already retained and ready for revival. Each of the above cues awakened specific bits of your previously registered and retained experience, and they were revived (retrieved) from your subconscious to your conscious awareness. All you needed was the correct reminder (retrieval cue), because your mind is, indeed, an associating machine! At this very moment your mind is literally brimming with millions of such immediately retrievable associations in the form of words, phrases, ideas, thoughts, names, facts, and other information of every conceivable description. You are an ocean of information composed of your own lifetime of experiences. All you need to do in order to get any of this information back out is to find and give your mind the correct retrieval cues. The instant action of association will do the rest. From here on, you will be learning how to deliberately implant powerful associations to surround the facts and materials you *want* to retain and revive later on. As for your past experience (before Memory Control training), you may still have difficulty reviving certain facts and other information you actually still possess, *unless* you know how to find the right retrieval cues. A later chapter, "The Retrieval of Lost Memories," will help you in this regard.

The exercise we did previously was designed to show you how efficiently association itself operates. The cue words BASKET, HOLIDAY, STOMACH, etc., were chosen at random, and any words that popped into your conscious mind were the result of pure associative action. Neither you nor I knew beforehand what they would be.

If, on the other hand, I gave the cue word CAT, it is probable that you might respond with the common associate DOG. Or TRUE with FALSE. Or MEAT with POTATOES. Or

PRIDE with JOY. Since all of these pairs have obvious or logical relationships, any one might bring on the other. But suppose I gave the cue MEATBALL. Do you think you might respond with ENVELOPE? Or, if I said, "PIANO," do you think you might respond with "FIRE"? Or, if I said the letter and number 0-98, would you respond with POLKA? Or PUSSYCAT with CORPORATION? Or TAXICAB with BOOKSHELF?

You'll probably agree that such unrelated responses would be surprising, to say the least. However, if these unlikely pairs of words *were* somehow previously associated in your mind, the force of association would still make them react as cues and responses. As you will see in a moment, this is a very interesting fact, with all kinds of possibilities. Any person can deliberately make associative connections between *any* items or ideas or facts so that they can work as cues and responses. It is this discovery, made more than 2,500 years ago, that will enable you to remember names and faces, phone numbers and who they belong to, facts and figures, and any and every other type of information you may have found impossible to remember.

When you meet a Mr. Ginkowski, and you want to somehow connect his name to his face so you can remember him, wouldn't you agree that his name and his face are an unlikely pair to associate and use as cue and response? HAM and EGGS are easy to use this way, as are HOT and COLD, FAST and SLOW, etc. But GINKOWSKI and a FACE? How in the world can this be done? Or, suppose you have an appointment with Ms. Appleton at 10:00 in the morning. How can you associate Ms. Appleton with *10:00 A.M.* so that one will remind you of the other? Such practical necessities as these and many others are the very things you will learn to remember at will in this book. And they are all based on what you are about to learn now. So pay attention and actively participate in the special exercise to follow. You will be creating associations (cues and responses) between six pairs of unlikely or unrelated ideas.

You are going to combine association with mental imagery

(picturing). They work together beautifully, and each enhances the other for better retention and retrieval. The following things are to be associated with each other. Just follow the directions:

1. **MEATBALL and ENVELOPE.** With a little imagination, this isn't difficult at all. What about an envelope full of meatballs? If you ever *did* see this, could you forget it? Then why not use it deliberately, for easy recall? Right now, in your mind's eye, see a white envelope full of steaming, delicious meatballs. Seal it and put it into your pocket for lunch. Strange? Yes, but that's one of the reasons you'll remember this association later. For now, never mind whether the associations are logical or fanciful. Either type will work, sometimes one better than the other. We'll be using both. Later, when you're more experienced with this and many other techniques, you can use the logical or the illogical, whichever is best for you or the kind of material you are memorizing.

   Back to the envelope full of steaming meatballs: See it and even savor the aroma if you like. See it now! ENVELOPE and MEATBALLS.

2. **PIANO and FIRE.** Another unlikely pair. We can use playful logic with this one. See and hear yourself playing "hot" music on the PIANO, which heats up so much it suddenly bursts into flames! See it now. Your piano is getting hotter and hotter, and there it goes—FIRE! Be sure to see this as well as you can, and even feel the heat, before you go on. PIANO and FIRE.

3. **O-98 (Letter O and number 98) and POLKA.** This may seem difficult at first to associate, but if you inject a little meaning into the picture, all will be well. Right now, mentally picture a squinting, wrinkled little old man in a white sweater with a big red 98 on it and *hear him* exclaiming to all, "*Oh*, I'm *98*, and I want to dance the POLKA!" See him and hear him say this *now*. O-98 and POLKA.

4. **PUSSYCAT and CORPORATION.** See a PUSSYCAT
with a big cigar in its mouth, at the head of the table,
leading a meeting of the CORPORATION. The
corporate pussycat! Or, if you know an executive in a
CORPORATION, see him or her with a black and white
PUSSYCAT, leading the meeting. Take the time to do
this now. PUSSYCAT and CORPORATION.

5. **TAXICAB and BOOKSHELF.** If you can think of a
logical association, use it, but be sure to put some kind of
action or exaggeration into your picture. Or, you can use
an imaginative association again and mentally picture a
small ceramic taxicab on the bookshelf, just beginning to
fall off the edge! It's up to you; see it *now*. Take your time;
see it as vividly as possible in your mind's eye. TAXICAB
and BOOKSHELF.

6. **IVORY SOAP and SCREWDRIVER.** Although these
seem unrelated, you can relate them very quickly by simply seeing a SCREWDRIVER repeatedly stabbing holes
into a bar of IVORY SOAP! See it now! IVORY SOAP
and SCREWDRIVER.

All right. Now, without looking at the previous items or
instructions, continue.

Look at the following retrieval cues, *one at a time*, and let
each one bring its response (the picture association you previously made) to your mind. As soon as you can, say the particular
response word or item. Here they are, in scrambled order:

1. PIANO
2. MEATBALL
3. 0-98
4. TAXICAB
5. IVORY SOAP
6. PUSSYCAT

I'm sure you did well, and you should be pleased with the

results. Now let's try it differently—backward! I will give the response words and see if you can come up with the original cue words. Cover up the previous list of six cues with your hand and proceed.

1. BOOKSHELF
2. FIRE
3. ENVELOPE
4. CORPORATION
5. SCREWDRIVER
6. POLKA

You can judge for yourself how well this works. You should have easily come up with all the right answers. You even might have recalled the correct words as soon as you saw each cue, even before the original picture you made came to mind! Such is the speed and accuracy of deliberately implanted associations, when done properly and vividly.

If you did miss one or two, go back, read the instructions, and do the exercises again. If you do *exactly as I direct*, you cannot fail. Yes, we used only six pairs of words (twelve items), but this number makes no difference. By using this technique you can achieve perfect results with a hundred or more such pairs of items. What you just did, of course, was to condition a set of responses in your own mind. In other words, you were putting the information into your memory in such a way that getting it back out again was easy.

It is highly unlikely that you could accomplish this as well as you just did, merely by reading over a list of such words once and then trying to recall them. If you don't believe this, have someone write a similar list for you. Then read it over once without picturing and see what happens. You will notice a sizable difference.

Many such tests have been done in university learning laboratories. Students who were instructed in the technique you just learned did from 100 percent to 800 percent better than those who didn't use such methods. Remember that we are working with some very basic principles. Never mind that they may seem overly simple. This is a plus. What is important at this point is that you get started in using an elementary memory technique *successfully*. The more sophisticated techniques you will learn later on are hardly more difficult than these, and they will work like magic, if you first master the basics.

Now we come to the whole point of the previous exercises. This is very important: Your mind is not only an associating machine. It is a *controllable* associating machine.

Do you realize what this means? It means that you have just successfully *controlled* your own memory. You did something that made your memory remember. You have exerted control over your initial registration of the information and the retrieval of that information. This is why I prefer the term *Memory Control* to *memory improvement*. As you learn to control your memory's input and output, your memory's performance—not your innate memory—improves dramatically.

You successfully exerted this kind of control a little earlier, with the Brain Chain technique in which you pictorially linked twelve different items in succession and then accurately recalled them in correct order. By using *controlled association* you forged successive links into a mental chain, after which each link worked as a retrieval cue, bringing the next one to mind. It was like setting off a string of mental firecrackers, each one igniting the next, producing a perfect Brain Chain reaction of retrieval.

Remember: *The basic unit in Memory Control is the retrieval cue.*

If, for any reason, you are not sure of what we have just covered, go back, re-read, and do the exercises again (including the Brain Chain section of Chapter 2, if necessary) before going on. The progress you make from here on depends on your understanding and success with the fundamentals we have covered up to this point.

Part II:
The Practical
Application of
Memory Control

> Memories may escape the action of will, may sleep a long time, but when stirred by the right influence, though that influence be light as a shadow, they flash into full stature and life with everything in place.
>
> *John Muir*

4

A Working Memory for Numbers: The Herold Number-Meaning Method

If you were offered a dime for each time someone forgot a phone number, you'd be a millionaire within a day. Even as you read these words, unbelievable numbers of people are forgetting not only phone numbers but license numbers, social security numbers, birthdates, street numbers and zip codes, shirt sizes, prices, model numbers, measurements, and statistics.

Because of this age-old memory blank for numbers, all sorts of methods and systems for remembering them have been devised and tried. Some have proved to be of limited use; others, of wider use, are too complicated. Nobody has come up with a practical solution for remembering numbers that is workable for most people. As a result, we usually resort to writing numbers down on paper. But what happens when those nasty little scribbles disappear? Without total recall or written reminders, many of us cannot consistently remember numbers.

In the following pages, I propose my own system for the retention and recall of numbers. No other book on memory to date has developed the ideas you are about to learn.

WHY NUMBERS SEEM DIFFICULT

First, it is important to understand why numbers seem so difficult to remember. The basic reason is that numbers have by themselves little meaning until they represent or refer to specific information. If something has no meaning for you, it has no interest. If it has no interest, it makes no impression. And if it makes no impression in the first place, how do you expect to remember it later? In the nutshell, that is the main problem with numbers.

As mentioned earlier, many number memory systems have been created over the centuries, all with limited effectiveness. And, unfortunately, people can't or won't spend the time and effort necessary to master and use these systems.

The method I have devised is surprisingly easy and is based on *natural associations*. By this I mean that *you* decide which meaning is most appropriate or natural for that particular number. In virtually all other number memory systems the meaning is basically dictated by the numbers themselves.

Perhaps the best feature of my method is its simplicity. You should be able to apply it almost immediately because you'll actually learn it by using it.

In Chapter 7, the lesson on names and faces, you will learn to give meaning to a name and then associate it with the face. Similarly, here you give meaning to any number and then associate it with whatever it represents. If it's a phone number, for instance, you mentally connect it with a person or place. If it's a price, you connect it with the particular item. This connection itself is a further meaning intensifier. Remember, MEANING is what makes numbers, names, or anything else stick in your mind.

NUMBERS AND MEANING

The question remains: *How* can we give meaning to numbers? Let's start with some simple examples. Basically, numbers are little more than abstract symbols or shapes on a piece of paper. But if you observe them closely, things begin to happen. Take a zero (0), for example. Really look at it for a moment and see what pops into your mind. What possible meaning could it have?

Your first reaction might be that zero is just plain nothing, literally. That's a start. Even "nothing" has some meaning, hasn't it? Or, you might say that zero reminds you of the *letter* O, because it looks the same. That's even better. You might think of words that rhyme with zero; for example, hero or Nero. If you put your imagination into play, the roundness of the zero reminds you of a doughnut, with its hole. Then it might remind you of a circle or a sphere. One thing leads to another, and many such *picturable* things spring into your mind. A planet, a globe, a light bulb, a hoop, a wheel, a round mirror on your wall, a clock, and so on.

The number of these natural associations is limited only by your imagination. You might think of Zero Mostel, the actor. Or a Japanese World War II fighter plane, the Zero. The sound of the word zero might even remind you of Xerox, for example. I think you get the idea.

For almost any number you can come up with such natural associations in exactly the same way. Sometimes you'll recognize the number's natural meanings or associations as soon as you see it or hear it. For example, 007 might make you think of James Bond. Or 66 might remind you of Phillips 66, or Route 66. If you see or hear the number 55, you might think of speed limit or someone you know who is age 55. The number 12 might remind you of a dozen of something. When you're a little more skillful with the method, the number 120 could easily mean a dozen doughnuts to you because you would quickly recognize these two separate possible "meaning units," 12 and 0, in the number 120.

For the number 30, you might think of the word month, because there are 30 days in a month. A number 6 or 8 might bring to mind a 6- or 8-cylinder car. In my memory seminars, when I ask five or six students to tell me what they see in a number, I usually get five or six different answers. Each individual has a gold mine of previously made natural associations. Everyone's experiences are different, so we all give different answers. The point is that with a little practice you can make these natural associations spring into your mind to help you salt away any numbers you want to be able to recall.

There will, of course, be plenty of times when you won't be able to see *any* meaning in a number, especially in the beginning. Here's where your creativity, aided by specific techniques for generating meaning where it doesn't seem to exist, comes into play.

The techniques discussed earlier for simple numbers also work for more complex numbers that do not easily call up a natural association or meaning. One of those specific techniques is simple rhyming (zero, hero). Now let's try the number 1045. As you look at it, does it bring anything specific to mind? If not, then *give* it meaning! Obviously the rhyme technique won't help here, so try another approach. A clock. In terms of time, 1045 becomes 10:45—either A.M. or P.M. If you're not a clock-watcher, perhaps an association with money will work for you. Use $10.45 or $1,045.

These rhyme, clock, and money ideas are only three of dozens of associative techniques you could easily use to assist you in generating meaning for numbers. Later I will provide specific ideas and techniques for quickly generating meaning for whatever numbers need special attention. Before long, as you continue to use this method, you'll be able to scan any number of reasonable size and either recognize at first sight the meaning already there or add meaning to it. One way or the other, you'll be *making* numbers meaningful, thus preparing them for future recall. This is called *coding* and it is the first step in a two-step method. The second step is *decoding*. The first step is easy; the second is even easier.

Before we go on, let's work with a few more examples. Take the number 9. This might bring baseball to mind (9 players on a team). How about 57? Does this mean anything to you? You might have thought of "Heinz 57 Varieties." You could easily picture a bottle of ketchup. What about the number 98? Many people think of the Model 98 Oldsmobile for this one. The Olds Model 88 could serve just as well for the number 88.

Now let's try a longer number. Here is a six-digit number.

0 9 5 7 9 8

Please look at this number carefully. What meanings does it already have for you? Instead of seeing a totally meaningless six-digit number, you should see some numbers or groups of numbers that remind you of something tangible and picturable. If this doesn't happen, look at the number below. It's the same six-digit number, but parts of it are underlined.

0 9 5 7 9 8

With the whole number broken into various units by the underscore, it should be easier to apply some meaning. No doubt you recognize these as numbers and meanings we've already discussed: The 0 could be a wheel, a doughnut, or whatever you want it to be. Similarly, the 9 could be a baseball. The 57 could be a big red bottle of Heinz ketchup, and the 98 could mean a shiny new Oldsmobile. Again, whatever *you* thought of instinctively is best for you.

Now for something important. Please do exactly as I ask.

1. Say to yourself, right now, each of the following numbers, *in order, just once.*

3 5 0 3 2 9 1 2 2 5

2. Now say the following sentence, *just once.*

Orson Welles gave me a bottle of freezing wine for Christmas.

3. Now look away from the page and try to recall the string of numbers you looked at.

4. Look away again and try to repeat the sentence you read.

How did you do? If you're like most people, the sentence was much easier to recall than the long number. The reason may be obvious, but it's very important to grasp at this point, because it forms the basis of the method you are now learning: *It is much easier to remember a sequence of words with meaning than it is to remember a sequence of numbers with no particular meaning.* Of course, you can see that this is just plain common sense. Words strung together form meaningful thoughts and sentences. Numbers strung together don't necessarily have meaning unless they refer to something specific. Now, if words or sentences are so much easier to remember than numbers (even at one glance, as you just proved to yourself), then why not use this fact to your advantage, to make remembering numbers easier? How can this be done? The answer is the description of the two-step method itself. This can be done by:

1. **Coding the numbers into meaningful words and sentences** so that your memory can grasp and hold onto this information;

2. **Decoding these words or sentences back into the original numbers** whenever you wish to recall them.

This, in essence, is the Number-Meaning Method. Now you are ready to begin to learn and use step one, coding or *sentencing*. The process of sentencing gives recallable meaning to the numbers and enables you to control their input and output in memory.

SENTENCING WITH NUMBERS

In the following pages I will take you step by step through this method of mentally managing numbers. One of the things that people complain the most about is forgetting telephone numbers. With this in mind, we will use telephone numbers as initial working examples with the method. You can use this method for telephone numbers of any length.

Let's start with the same long number you looked at a few minutes ago. This time, however, it is in the form of a ten-digit phone number:

3 5 0 - 3 2 9 - 1 2 2 5

You could try to find meaning for each individual number, but this would take too long. And thus the sentence would be unnecessarily long as well. Try, instead, to work with more than one number at a time as you go along. In general, grouping or "chunking" two, three, four or more digits together to form a unit of meaning is more efficient: it reduces the time to program the numbers into your mind, and it is easier to decode later on. Now look at the above number again, but try putting the first two digits together. Does the number 35 trigger any particular meaning in your mind? Assuming it doesn't, try working with the first three digits, 350. Notice the zero! By this time a zero should trigger some meaning in your mind—a doughnut, a circle, a wheel, actor Zero Mostel, etc. Or the zero might remind you of the *letter* O. As one thought leads to another, that round O reminds you of another actor, a very *round* actor, Orson Welles. He's so round he could easily weigh at least *350* pounds. That's it—you've got his number! From this moment on, *350* represents Orson Welles. He is the "meaning unit" for that number. See him now, for a moment, in your mind's eye. See him on a scale, if you like; he weighs in at exactly 350 pounds. You don't always have to picture the meaning, but doing so adds staying power to the impression by intensifying the meaning.

It's important to keep in mind that the association you just contrived works two ways. When you think of Orson Welles, 350 comes to mind and vice versa. One of these two things instantly reminds you of the other. This is a *positive action reminder* because you deliberately made the *specific* association.

So far, so good. The next three digits in our number are 3, 2, and 9. Again, use whatever response pops into your mind. The number 329 may not trigger anything, so try the first *two* digits, 32. Aha! The freezing point of water is 32 degrees Fahrenheit. Next is the number 9. The first thing this triggers for me is a rhyme: wine. Put the two together and you can "freeze" the wine in your mind's eye. Even better, picture Orson Welles holding a bottle of freezing wine.

3 5 0   3 2   9
ORSON WELLES - FREEZING WINE

Remember, the way to reinforce this association is to *picture* Orson Welles holding a bottle of freezing wine. Incidentally, if you've seen Orson Welles in the TV commercial in which he pours a glass of wine, this association is even more meaningful.

So far we've coded more than half of the phone number with recallable meaning. The remaining numbers to work with are 1, 2, 2, and 5. The first thing that grabs my attention is the 12 at the beginning, which immediately makes me think of a dozen of something. The 25 that follows could be 25¢, a quarter. Put together, this gives you a dozen quarters. Now see if you can work with a larger grouping, perhaps all four digits at once. What about Christmas? December 25, is often written *12/25*. This allows you to see Orson Welles as a big, round Santa, handing you a bottle of freezing wine for Christmas. Here is the nearly complete Number-Meaning Graph:

3 5 0   3 2   9   1 2 2 5
ORSON WELLES FREEZING WINE CHRISTMAS

You have now broken a ten-digit phone number into only three meaning units, for easy remembering. Technically, there are four chunks if you consider the 32 and the 9 separately. But the phrase *freezing wine* easily makes this only *one* meaning unit, so why not simplify it for practical purposes? Incidentally, the very idea of freezing wine aids the recall process because it is so unlikely.

Now, for easy decoding and recall, you simply use those three "number chunks" (meaning units) with the addition of a few "connector" words to make a complete sentence. Here is the complete Number-Meaning Graph.

> 3 5 0   3 2 9
> *Orson Welles* (gave me a bottle of) *freezing wine*
>   1 2 2 5
> (for) *Christmas.*

A little while ago you proved to yourself that you could recall a sentence with greater ease and accuracy than a ten-digit number. And now you have made it easy to remember a ten-digit number by associating it with a sentence—without the ineffective drill of repetition. Most people would attempt to remember a long number by repeating all or parts of the number over and over again. But, as with most rote memorization tasks, the "memorized" material quickly fades from the mind, and there's no way to be sure you can recall it again.

With the natural associations of the Number-Meaning Method, however, you actually remember long or short numbers *with virtually no repetition.* Instead, you only think or say to yourself *once or twice*, a meaningful phrase or sentence that contains the complete number in coded sentence form. You never have to "memorize" the number itself. This is what I mean by the phrase *memory without memorizing.*

You have completed step one of the method, the *input.* You have coded meaning into the numbers. Now you are ready for step two, the *output*, in which you will decode the sentence to get the original numbers. Coding is the input, or registration.

Decoding is the output, or retrieval.

Let's begin step two. If you've followed all the instructions to this point, you should have no difficulty in recalling the phone number we've been processing with this method. *All you have to do is think of the Orson Welles sentence you just completed.* Do it now, word by word, and merely decode it as you go along to get the original numbers.

You have now registered, retained, and retrieved a ten-digit telephone number with this simple sentencing technique. At this point any number with fewer than ten digits will be even easier to handle. Numbers with more than ten digits are handled in exactly the same way.

Later, I'll teach you how to connect any phone number (or any other number) to the person, company, or place it represents. The sentencing technique is really a mental holding device that holds the numbers in proper sequence in your mind. If you want to remember the number for a long period of time, all you have to do is reinforce it occasionally, simply by repeating the particular phrase or sentence once or twice, mentally decoding that sentence before you dial the number or use it in some other way. Such use is the best reinforcement.

With a little practice you will develop speed in sentencing, and it will become a very handy asset. If you happen to be driving with the radio on, and you hear a phone number or other number or address you want to remember (without pulling over to stop and write it down) you can code it and retain it. Later, when you have a chance, you can decode it and use it, or write it down if you wish.

The following listing of numbers and meanings will further clarify the use of meaning units with numbers. Remember, these are just a few of the tens of thousands of such possibilities! Again, you should use whatever associations you feel are best. The list begins with some rhymes for numbers, to remind you that rhyming is a fast and efficient mental holding device and retrieval cue.

RANDOM NUMBERS AND SOME SUGGESTED MEANINGS

A Few Rhymes

(Some of the rhymes below are not perfect, but they are close enough to work.)

1: bun, sun, gun, fun, done, pun, stun, run
2: glue, shoe, crew, moo, do, due, sue, blew, blue
3: tree, she, ski, free, be, bee, tea, tee
4: door, floor, score, more, core, store, boar
5: dive, drive, live, hive, jive, arrive, five, chive
6: bricks, sticks, chicks, nicks, fix, picks, ticks
7: heaven, leaven, Kevin, Bevin, Previn
8: gate, plate, date, rate, mate, state, crate, freight
9: wine, dine, fine, pine, stein, mine, sign
0: hero, Nero, zero, De Niro
10: hen, den, pen, glen, men, ten, zen
12: shelf, elf
13: flirting
14: courting
15: lifting, shifting, drifting
18: mating, dating, waiting, plaiting
19: winding, binding, finding
20: Benny, Jenny, Kenny, Lenny, many, penny, bunny, honey, funny, sunny, money (if you pronounce 20 as "twunty," as many people do.)
30: dirty, Gerty, flirty
40: shorty, Morty
50: nifty, shifty, thrifty
60: Trixie, Dixie, pixie
70: heavenly
80: Haiti, lady, shady
90: fine tea

Numbers That Suggest Their Own Meanings

0: letter O, circle, wheel, doughnut, globe, light bulb, clock

1: 1 God, 1 nation, Route 1, a dollar bill

2: 2 eyes, ears, hands; a couple; twins; 2 of anything

3: 3M, triplets, 3 of anything

4: quadruplets, "fore!" (golf), car (4 wheels), 4 of anything

5: quintuplets, a nickel, a fifth, a hand (5 fingers), $5, 5 Great Lakes

6: 1/2 dozen, a 6-shooter, a 6-pack, 6th floor, 6 cylinders (a car)

7: 7-up, a week (7 days), 7 wonders of world, 7 o'clock

8: 8 cylinders, octagon, octopus,

9: baseball, (9 lives) a cat

10: a dime, a $10 bill, 10 percent, 10:00 P.M.

11: parallel bars, a football team, channel 11

12: noon, midnight, a dozen, a foot (12 inches), a year (12 months)

13: Friday the 13th, a black cat, a ladder, the 13th floor (superstition)

14: a valentine (February 14), Columbus (1492)

15: a dime and a nickel, a 15¢ cigar

16: "sweet 16," 1 pound (16 ounces)

20: a $20 bill

21: 21-gun salute, a card game/blackjack, voting age, 3 weeks

22: Washington's birthday (February 22), a 22-caliber gun

24: 2 dozen, a day (24 hours)

25: a quarter, 1/4 pound

28: February (28 days)

29: the Depression ('29), leap year (February 29)

30: a month, somebody's age

32: freezing point of water (32 degrees Fahrenheit)

36: a yard, a yardstick (36 inches)
38: a police revolver
39: Jack Benny (age "39"), the movie *39 Steps*
40: the book *Life Begins at 40*
41: Pearl Harbor ('41)
45: 45, 33, and 78 rpm record turntable speeds, 45-degree angle, a gun
49: 1849 California gold rush
50: United States, 50¢, $50, half century
52: a year (52 weeks), cards (52 in a deck)
55: speed limit (55 mph)
57: Heinz 57 Varieties: ketchup, beans, etc.
60: 2 months (60 days), age 60
61: 1961—first manned space flight
66: Phillips 66, Route 66
88: Oldsmobile (model 88)
98: Oldsmobile (model 98)
007: James Bond
100: Great Books, a $100 bill
107: 10 bottles of 7-Up
212: boiling point of water (212 degrees Fahrenheit)
360: a full circle (360 degrees)
444: 444 days captivity, U.S. hostages in Iran
500: Fortune 500 companies, Indianapolis 500
710: 7 dimes, 7 hens (rhyme), 71 doughnuts, $710
711: dice, "7-come-11"
727: a jetliner
747: a jetliner
911: police emergency phone number

Longer numbers may coincide with historic dates or other familiar figures, making it unnecessary to break them down.

1492: Columbus
1600: White House (1600 Pennsylvania Avenue)
1776: Declaration of Independence

1984: Orwell's famous book *1984*
2001: the movie *2001*
2020: 20/20 (normal vision)
5,280: feet in a mile
20,000: famous book *20,000 Leagues Under the Sea*
25,000: distance (in miles) around the earth
186,000: light bulb (the speed of light in miles per second)

Any date, formula, statistic, or other familiar number can be used. It is especially effective to use associations that call up *pictures*. For example, 2020 could mean eyeglasses (20/20). Or picture a light bulb for 186,000 (the speed of light in miles per second).

The list of numbers that have some inherent meaning is endless and limited only by your knowledge, experience, and imagination.

Now that you know the fundamentals, we can proceed much faster. Let's work another example or two of sentencing. Here is a seven-digit phone number, the type we use most often:

3 9 1 - 1 1 2 1

Suppose nothing occurs to you as meaning for the three-digit exchange, 391. In that case, just take the 39. Unless you're very young, this number could easily remind you of the perennial age "39" of the late comedian Jack Benny. Or you might think of the movie *39 Steps*. If you're a nostalgia buff, you'll recognize this film right away. Now you must code the 1. To save time, quickly *rhyme it* and use the verb *won*. Here's how you would say it or think it so far:

3 9   1
JACK BENNY WON

Don't write it, think it! Don't use a pencil unless you have to. Pretty soon you won't even think of using a pencil.

Next come the last four numbers: 1, 1, 2, and 1. A quick scan shows that it won't be difficult to code them two at a time. The number 11 always reminds me of football (11 men on a team). See it as a football. Next is 21. If you've ever been to Las Vegas, you know what that means. Blackjack! Here's how you turn it into a complete sentence.

3 9   1   1 1   2 1
Jack Benny won a *football* playing *blackjack*

A phone number is useless unless you know to whom it belongs. So you must connect the sentence you just coded to a person, a place, or a thing. Suppose this number belongs to your physician, Dr. Jones. You just put him into the action:

Jack Benny won a football playing *blackjack* with *Dr. Jones.*

If you prefer, you could put Dr. Jones at the beginning of the sentence:

Dr. Jones and *Jack Benny* both *won* a *football* playing *blackjack*

You could even put Dr. Jones in the middle somewhere.

Jack Benny won a *football* from *Dr. Jones,* playing *blackjack.*

The important point is to *see* your doctor and Jack Benny clearly in your mind's eye, playing blackjack. In this way, when you think of Dr. Jones, he *or* his name will remind you instantly of the tailor-made sentence you created just for him.

This kind of sentence may seem fanciful, but remember that the very improbability of the scene you conjure up makes it a strong memory aid. For better or worse, the human mind remembers the outstanding and the unusual far better and longer than the ordinary and the routine. Remember that this system will work with any kind of sentence you can remember.

Now, say the following sentence a couple of times until you can repeat it easily without looking at it. Then run it through your mind and decode it.

Jack Benny won a *football* playing *blackjack* with *Dr. Jones.*

Now, let's work with an eight-digit number that could be a serial number, an identification number, or an account number.

1 0 3 6 1 3 1 2

Try to code these numbers at least two at a time. The 10 could be a dime, $10 dollars, the movie *Ten* or a tent (a picturable, though imperfect, rhyme). The number 36 could represent 36th street, 3 dozen of something, 36 minutes, March 6th (3/6), and so on. The first thing that I think of for the number 13 is a black cat or a ladder (superstition). The number 12 could be a clock (12 o'clock), or noon, or midnight. We already have more than enough picture symbols for those numbers to code meaning into a workable sentence.

10	36	13	12

$10 YARDSTICK BLACK CAT MIDNIGHT

Say the name you need to associate with that number—a name on a charge account, for example—is Simmons. If you know a Simmons, you can mentally visualize him or her in whatever action you choose in your sentencing. Otherwise, if the name Simmons means nothing to you, you can give it meaning. Just think of or visualize a Simmons brand mattress. From then on, when you need the Simmons account number, you could run a sentence like the following through your mind and decode it quickly:

10

On a *Simmons's* mattress is a *ten-dollar*

36   13   12

yardstick to chase *black cats* at *midnight.*

Variations could include "*Simmons* has a *ten-dollar yardstick*, and he chases *black cats* at *midnight.*" Or "For *$10 Simmons* will give you his *yardstick* to chase *black cats* at *midnight.*" Any of these, or any other sentence that works for you, would be just as good or better. Now, whenever you pull out Simmons's account card, you run through the phrase or sentence you have created for him or her and decode it into the correct account number. If your job includes working with many account numbers, you could easily speed up your work by having key account numbers and names in mind at all times, using this handy mental shorthand.

I mentioned before that many of my memory students come up with cleverly appropriate sentences for numbers that are called out by the class. Here is how one student programmed the number 10317941 using only two chunks:

10/31/79   4/1

Halloween, '79 and *April Fool's Day!*

Now can you see why I recommend *chunking* whenever you can.

This brings us to the important subject of learning specific ways to help code meaning into numbers. There will be times, especially when you are new at this, when you cannot recognize any meaning inherent in the number, and you also cannot seem to establish any meaning of your own. By using the following ideas as springboards, you will be able to put meaning into the numbers.

PATTERN RECOGNITION

Occasionally you may notice another kind of meaning in a

number you observe, in the form of a recognizable *pattern*. This pattern could be a powerful memory aid to help you recall the number easily. For example, if you see sequences or patterns like 3 6 9 12—or 1 2 4 5 7 8 10 11, 1 5 10 15 20, 4 5 6 7, or 9 7 5 3 1 or other variations—use them! They are workable holding devices that the numbers themselves provide for you. The trick is to observe them. Remember that you see with the eye, but you observe with the mind.

Numbers instantly express amounts and measurements, whether they apply to time, money, distance, speed, age, weight, or anything else. That's what numbers are for. But the beautiful part of the Number-Meaning Method is that numbers that were originally intended to express or represent such specific categories can instantly be transferred to whatever other category you want them to represent. The purpose, of course, is to code meaning, by natural association, into that number, for far easier recall than the original category itself provided.

For example, a lawyer's phone number, 445-6905, could easily be coded, by picturing him as age 44, 5 foot 6, and a bill from him for $905 per visit. We started with one category, a phone number, and instantly changed it into three completely different categories—age, height, and money. The point is that you can use any category you choose to make difficult numbers more easily memorable.

There's no end to the various categories and subdivisions you can use. They are all control techniques for making meaningless numbers meaningful. To clarify this further, here is a listing of ten categories, with illustrations:

1. **TIME:** You can code numbers into units of time. The number 431 quickly becomes 4:31. Similarly, 1215 is 12:15, 205 is 2:05, 1043 is 10:43, and 105 is 1:05.
2. **DATES:** You can code many numbers in this way. If you have difficulty thinking of a meaning unit for 623, you can code it as June 23 (6/23). In the same way, 1102 might be November 2 (11/02). On the other hand, if you see a number you *recognize* as a signifi-

cant date, you can code it as such immediately, using the meaning of that date: 1492 means Columbus. I'd recognize 1113 (11/13) as my birthday. You can do the same with yours. If I observe that a number matches my wife's or children's birthdays, I code it as such then and there, visualizing *them* in the sentencing. Any date that you already know, *and recognize when you see it,* can be used for coding numbers of all sizes. For example, 214 is a valentine (2/14).

3. **ADDRESSES:** The same is true for this category: The numbers you already know—your home or work address or any other important address—can be used in this way if you're on the lookout for them! For example, if your address is 4126 Elm, any 4126 that you come across can instantly be coded and visualized as your house.

4. **STREETS and ROUTE NUMBERS:** Numbered streets such as 47th St., 63rd St., 159th St., etc., can be used, as well as Route 1, 43, 66, 94, 294, etc. Whichever association springs to mind from your driving or traveling experience can be used.

5. **DISTANCE:** Use any unit that measures distance. For instance, 488 would be 488 miles, 5010 could be 5,010 miles, and 109 1/2 would mean 109 1/2 miles. If you happen to remember that 25,000 miles is the distance around the earth, you could use this association and picture the globe.

6. **SPEED:** An obvious example is to associate 55 with the speed limit. Any number could become miles per hour, if you decide to use it as such. 25, 35, 40, 50, 80, 90—any one you like. Another big chunk you might recall from science is 240,000 miles, the distance from the earth to the moon.

7. **TEMPERATURE:** We already associated 32 with 32 degrees Fahrenheit (freezing point of water) and 212 as 212 degrees (boiling point of water). If you come

across 98.6, associate it with normal body temperature. There are also wind speed categories and barometric pressure readings. Use any kind of number that has meaning for you.

8. **RADIO or TV NUMBERS:** Use channels 2, 3, 5, 11, 44, 55, etc. Let your favorite performer be your meaning unit if he or she appears on a certain channel, or just picture your TV set to represent that number. The term "10-4" is a well-known signoff signal over CB and police radios (104 = 10-4). Are you beginning to appreciate the versatility and practicality of this Number-Meaning technique?

9. **MONEY:** This is one of the easiest categories to use because everybody is familiar with money. Again, any number can be thought of as a price, cost, budget figure, sales volume, profit, loss, balance, overdraft, credit-card limit, or just a simple present (visualize it) you just gave somebody that cost exactly the amount represented by the number you're coding. We used money in a recent example: "On a *Simmons* mattress is a *ten-dollar yardstick* for chasing *black cats* at *midnight.*" What number does this sentence bring back? Decode it!

10. **SIMILAR SOUNDS:** This is an especially easy and workable technique to code numbers quickly for sentencing. Just about any number that you can think up a similar sound for (especially if you can picture it) will work. A few examples for numbers were listed earlier. Here are a few more:

20: plenty, friendly
21: Honey bun, Tunney won
22: Bunny Lou, funny stew
23: honey free
24: money for, too sore
25: to dive, funny dive
26: two sticks, plenty bricks

27: to heaven, sunny heaven
28: do great, funny mate
29: blue wine, sunny shine
30: dirty/birdie, 3030 = hurdy-gurdy
31: dirty fun, 30 buns
32: sea blue, birdie flew
33: freebee, sturdy bee
34: tree door, dirty boar
35: see live, flirty jive
36: be sick, 30 bricks
37: free Kevin, birdie heaven
38: she ate, Gerty's date/Ferde's late
39: we sign, sturdy pine
40: more oats, shorty
530: live birdie
3888: flirty Kate ate late

We could go on and on with such examples. They are limited only by your imagination. The ten categories listed for generating meaning for numbers are only a few of many.

Here is a little rhyming memory jogger for bringing a few quick categories to mind when you see them:

TIME, PRICE, DATE
AGE, HEIGHT, WEIGHT

Using the knowledge you have so far with all the techniques, spend some time with the following exercises in coding and retrieving numbers. The funnier, more unusual, or more striking you make your phrases and sentencing, the better you'll remember them. Again, the first things that pop into your mind in response to a number are often the best. See it all happening in your mind's eye as you go along.

As an overall reminder, before you begin, here's a quick, step-by-step review of the method.

Meaning Joggers	NUMBER	WRITE IN MEANINGS YOU RECOGNIZED OR CREATED YOURSELF:
TIME		
PRICE	4	_____
DATE	9	_____
AGE	15	_____
HEIGHT	20	_____
WEIGHT	42	_____
MONEY		
DISTANCE		
SPEED		
TEMPERATURE		
RADIO-TV CHANNELS		
SIZES		

Some ideas you might have used for meaning for the above numbers:

For 4: "rhymes" with *door* or *fork* or *ford*; 4 wheels, quadruplets

For 9: *9 lives; rhymes with wine, dine, sign;* baseball (9 on team)

For 15: 15¢ cigar, candy bar; dime and nickel; 15 pounds

For 20: 2 dimes, a $20 bill, Route 20, 20 mph, 20 minutes

Meaning Joggers	NUMBER	WRITE IN MEANINGS YOU RECOGNIZED OR CREATED YOURSELF:
RHYMES		*For 42:* age 42, rhymes with *more glue*, 4-2 *for you and door-blue*; 4 feet 2; 42¢; April 2 (4/2)
ROUTES	312	
MODEL NUMBERS	495	
	687	

Some ideas you might have used for these 3-digit numbers:

For 312: area code 312, 3 dozen (3-12), 3−1 = 2, 312 miles, 3:12 P.M.

For 495: 49 $5 bills, '49 gold rush— *"49ers were alive"* (which rhymes with 5).

For 687: *"68 was heaven,"* June of 87 (6/87), six 87-year-olds, "between 6 and 8 is 7," "Fixate Kevin." (Fix-ate Kevin = 687 rhyme)

Meaning Joggers	NUMBER
Any Number You Already Know With Meaning	
Birthdate	213
Address	4950

Meaning Joggers	NUMBER	WRITE IN MEANINGS YOU RECOGNIZED OR CREATED YOURSELF:
TIME		
PRICE		Now, here is a seven-digit phone number composed of the previous numbers, 213 and 4950, or 213-4950. Code these numbers into a phrase or sentence using whatever meaning you wrote in above or any other meaning you think of.
DATE		
AGE		
HEIGHT		
WEIGHT	213-4950	
MONEY		One phrase might be a Hardware Store phone number:
DISTANCE		2 13 4 9 50
SPEED		*Two ladders for $9.50*
TEMPERATURE		(Ladder could represent the number 13, due to superstitions about ladders and 13.)
RADIO-TV CHANNELS		2 13 4 95 0
SIZES		Or: On *February 13,* I had *four* 95-cent *doughnuts.*
		(doughnut shop phone number)

NUMBER	WRITE IN MEANINGS YOU RECOGNIZED OR CREATED YOURSELF:
Meaning Joggers	
RHYMES	
ROUTES	
MODEL NUMBERS	213 Or: At 2:13 A.M., I won *$4,950!* (Casino phone number)
Any Number You Already Know With Meaning	

With a little practice now and then, this simple process becomes earlier than it may seem to you at this moment. Remember that any worthwhile skill takes a bit of initial effort. Here are two more phone numbers for you to code into a phrase or sentence:

Piano store phone number: _____

Birthdate   388-5057 _____

License number: _____

Address   12741 _____

For the phone number 388-5057, here are a few coding ideas:

3   88 (keys)   50   57
1. Only *3 pianos* in the *states*, all covered with *ketchup!*
2. Joe has *3 pianos, 50¢* each, covered with *ketchup.*
3. I found *$388* in *half-dollars* on *57*th St.
4. *Three* Olds *88*s crossed the *United States* in *57* minutes!
5. *$3.88* buys *50* bottles of *ketchup!*
6. The *38*th *plate* of *nifty ketchup.* (rhymes: plate = 8, nifty = 50)

The license number 127.41 could be coded along some of the following ideas:

1. *12/7/41*, Pearl Harbor invasion by Japan. (DATE)
2. I drank a *dozen 7*-Ups on *April Fool's Day* (4/1). (DATE)
3. *Twelve 74*-year-olds in only *1* room. (AGE)
4. I do my daily *dozen* at *7:41* A.M. *(TIME)*
5. *On 1/27*, my car had *41* million miles. (DISTANCE)
6. Johnson lost *127* pounds in *41* days. (WEIGHT AND TIME)
7. *Twelve sevens* are bigger than *four ones.* (MEASUREMENT)
8. A *dozen* dresses, size *7*, for a *41*-year-old woman. (SIZE and AGE)
9. *12 divided into 74* is *1* headache! (MEASUREMENT)
10. *Once*, in Car *274*, I *won* the race. (ID NUMBER)
11. *12/74* was *one* month I'll never forget. (DATE)
12. At *12* midnight on *July 4*, we were *one*. (DATE)

1. Observe the numbers carefully. Try to recognize any meaning the number might already hold for you. It might be a date like 1492, or it might be part of an address or a business statistic. Use your pencil, if you like, for this practice. Make your own Number-Meaning Graphs the way we've done them so far. Group numbers when possible for easier coding and decoding.
2. If you don't recognize any usable meaning already in the number, put your imagination into play to come up with meanings of your own choosing. Examples: Weight: Orson Welles = 350. States: 50 = U.S. Money: 50 = $50. Time: 431 = 4:31. Person/Age: 39 = Jack Benny.

The table on pages 45-49 has some numbers for you to work with in coding and decoding. If you need help in creating meaning for numbers that do not already have recognizable meaning, use the meaning joggers in the left-hand column or the random numbers and suggested meanings listed earlier.

Now that you have had a little practice with the Number-Meaning Method, take another look at some sentencing examples we did originally. You can use them, along with the examples in the table, as models in the sentencing exercises you are about to begin. Here are a few of our originally coded sentences:

Ten-Digit Telephone Number
350-329-1225: *Orson Welles* gave me a bottle of *freezing wine* for *Christmas*.

A Doctor's Phone Number
391-1121: Dr. Jones's friend, *Jack Benny, won* a *football* playing *blackjack*.

An Eight-Digit Identification or Serial Number
10317941: *Halloween* '79 and *April Fool's* Day (10/31/79).

An Eight-Digit Account Number
10361312: Simmons has a *ten-dollar yardstick* to chase *black cats* at *midnight.*

A Lawyer's Telephone Number
445-6905: My lawyer is *44, 5* foot *6,* and charges *$905* per visit.

YOUR FIRST PRACTICAL USE OF
THE NUMBER-MEANING METHOD

Now you can put to practice what you have learned. The following is a list of people and things that are important to you. Take your time and enjoy this exercise. Just look for meaning already in the numbers or add meaning of your own in coding sentences for these numbers.

Your Car's License Plate Number or Your ID Number

(write it here:) _____

Now code it into a phrase or sentence: _____

_____

(Note: If you already know your car's license plate number by heart, or the other numbers to follow, use different numbers for these exercises.)

Your Doctor's Telephone Number

(number) _____

Phrase or sentence: _____

_____

Police, Fire, or Other Emergency Number

(number)_____

Phrase or sentence:_____

_____

Your Social Security or Other ID Number

(number)_____

Phrase or sentence:_____

_____

A Friend's Phone Number

(number)_____

Phrase or sentence:_____

_____

Other Important Number

(number)_____

Phrase or sentence:_____

_____

HOW TO KEEP THESE NUMBERS IN MIND

Now that you have coded the above numbers into meaningful sentences, remembering them is easy when you follow these three simple rules:

1. Select no more than one or two of the above numbers to commit to memory for now. Don't rush; you can memorize the others one by one later on.
2. Say the completed phrase or sentence a few times until you can repeat it easily without looking at it.
3. Mentally decode the sentence to get the original numbers. It is easy, as you will see. Take your time at first. Speed will come quickly with a bit of practice. All you have to do to remember the number is to use it now and then. Just say it to yourself occasionally, the sentence and then the

decoded number. Every time you must call your friend, or doctor, or use your Social Security number, just think of your tailor-made sentence and decode it for use. After you do this often enough, you won't need the sentence at all.

SUMMARY

The three basic principles that underlie the Number-Meaning Method are:

1. Numbers are easier to register, retain, and recall if the numbers *themselves* call forth natural associations or if they are deliberately imbued with recallable meaning.
2. Associating new information with something you already know is how all learning takes place. In this way, taking meaningless numbers and imbuing them with meaning for you completes the cycle of learning and remembering.
3. You accomplish steps 1 and 2 above simply by coding number meanings *you* choose into phrases or sentences; then you decode them to get the original numbers.

You are now in a position to manage your mind's processing of numerical information for retention and recall. With this method of control, you effectively *register* the number in your mind, effectively *retain* it through reinforcement by associative meaning and occasional use, and then reliably *retrieve* the number with simple decoding of a sentence retrieval cue.

Keep in mind that remembering is a *skill*. As with any worthwhile skill, you crawl before you walk, and you walk before you run. But when you reach the running stage, the benefits are more than worth the initial effort, and mastery becomes its own reward.

While this method is still new to you, take every opportunity to use it for any specific number that you feel should be committed to memory. At first, take the time to write the numbers down to observe them and discover ways to code them with appropriate meaning. With such use of the Number-Meaning Method will come confidence and speed, and before you know it, you will be able to code and decode number meanings in your mind without needing pencil and paper.

By managing your memory for numbers, you will be managing your time more efficiently. Looking up certain numbers repeatedly is time consuming and wasteful. The minutes you save by committing certain important numbers easily to memory will add up to significant blocks of time in the long run. For emergency use, important numbers you can instantly recall are far more valuable than those you have to look up.

Not to be overlooked are the genuine fringe benefits of using the Number-Meaning Method. Besides remembering numbers better than you ever did before, you will also be increasing your powers of observation, imagination, and creativity.

5

Farewell to Forgetfulness!

At one time or another, almost everybody experiences the frustration and stress caused by forgetting where something is. Usually, this is called *absentmindedness* or *forgetfulness*, and it can happen with car keys (or the car!), important documents, jewelry, important notations, in the office, at home, anywhere. And it usually does. It's at moments like these that you wonder, "What's the matter with me? I just put it someplace a few minutes ago. Am I losing my mind?"

Fortunately, this exasperating little human dilemma is relatively easy to prevent when you know how. There is a good reason for using the word *absentminded* to describe what actually happens in such a situation: Your mind was literally absent when you put the item wherever you put it. At the exact moment of that mysterious action, your mind was on something else, something more important to you, and you just didn't pay attention to what you were doing. So it's really not at all surprising that you "forgot" where you put it. What *is* surprising is that most of us expect to remember where we put such things, in spite of the fact that we don't mentally register the action in the first place. If you never really consciously knew where you put it, how can you recall it? The fact is that nobody can remember anything that is not actually learned or "known" in the first place. The classic example is not being able to remember someone's name after having met the person two minutes ago. If you didn't pay attention to that name, you didn't learn it in the first place. So you didn't really "forget" it, you just never knew it. The same thing can happen when you can't "remember" a shirt size or a phone number that originally went in one ear and out the other. You can't "forget" what you never knew.

It is human nature not to pay attention to things that are not important at the moment. It stands to reason that when you put something down—a pencil, a pack of cigarettes, a letter, or even a diamond ring—it just may not seem important at that moment. For example, let's say you put your wristwatch on the table; you put a pair of scissors on the chair; you put a shopping list on the gas range; you put your glasses on the sink; you put a letter on your bed; you put a deck of cards on the TV set; you put your briefcase in the closet; you put a book down on the typewriter; you put a ruler on the piano; and you put some dollar bills on the dryer.

I have just given you ten things, which were put in ten different places. I didn't ask you to pay particular attention or to try to remember anything. Because of this, it shouldn't be too surprising if you can't recall where many (or any) of these objects were placed. Now, *without looking at the preceding paragraph*, try this: The following list contains the ten items. As you look at each one, try to remember where it was just put.

The ruler
The shopping list
The glasses
The briefcase
The dollar bills
The watch
The scissors
The letter
The cards
The book

How did you do? Much difficulty should be expected because of the casual way in which these items and locations were originally presented. The point is that such casual mention is very similar to the way people put things down without really paying attention to what they are doing. This casual, absentminded attitude can easily create a blank as far as your memory is concerned. You just can't blame your memory for "forgetting" things that you never registered. Even geniuses are subject to this basic law of learning and remembering. You only remember what you learn, and you have learned only what you can remember.

It all comes back to the "Three Rs of Remembering": registration, retention, and retrieval. It's important to keep in mind that the *quality* of your original registration (learning) is what determines how well you *retain* and *retrieve* it later, whether it's an item you "misplaced," a person's name, a date, something you read, or anything else.

The question is, then, *how* can you improve the quality of your registration? The answer lies in the method I'm about to teach you. This method will also teach you how to remember where you put things. Actually, you will learn two different techniques. Both are quick and simple, and both work immediately.

Although paying attention to what you are doing is an important initial step for learning and remembering, there is much more to it. As you know, you can pay attention to something and still forget it later on. Securely registering something in your mind involves not only your attention but other important things as well, things you must actively do in order to enhance and strengthen that registration.

HOW TO REMEMBER WHERE YOU PUT THINGS

1. The Talking Technique

This technique will seem deceptively simple but it is a technique you must *use* to realize how well it actually works.

At the very moment you are putting something in a place, *say to yourself* (mentally or, preferably, out loud) something along the following lines: "I am at this moment putting these car keys on the top shelf of the bookcase. You'd better be there, little car keys, when I come to get you."

You will find that this simple procedure works because it counteracts the absentmindedness that prevents you from remembering. Instead of your mind being "absent" when you put the keys down, you deliberately create awareness and attention at that exact moment. You are not only fully aware of what you are doing; you are also further reinforcing that awareness in three different ways: You *see* where you put those keys. You are *thinking* about what you are doing. And by talking to yourself you also *hear* what you're saying. With this kind of multiple sensory input, you cannot help but register what you're doing at that moment, a hundred times more powerfully than if you just casually put those keys on the shelf without thought or purpose.

You don't, of course, have to use the exact wording given in the example. Just be sure you *describe to yourself what it is that you are doing at that precise moment and then talk to the object itself for further reinforcement.* This method is so simple and effective that many people don't believe it works or just forget to use it. Don't make this mistake. Use it when you know that you want to remember where you place or put a particular item. This simple method requires no practice or study. It just works.

Long-Term Remembering

With further reinforcement the talking technique can work well beyond a twenty-four-hour period. If it is important to be able to remember where you put those rings, documents, or keys six months or a year from now, then use the following reinforcement procedure. It will greatly enhance the method's power, effectiveness, and durability. Remember William James's principle that the secret of a good memory is to form diverse and multiple associations. The answer lies in those words. The more associations that surround a fact in your mind, the more retrieval cues you have to bring that fact back to mind. Therefore, for longer-term remembering, invest more time in the talking method at the moment you put something important away. Reinforce your attentiveness by not only thinking or talking to yourself as before, *but by citing every reason you can think of* to remember where you are placing the item. This Diverse and Multiple Association Registration Technique thus cross-indexes your memory file with many extra cues for future retrieval. All of this extra thought and reasoning creates a web of associations and meanings, which are transferred to your long-term memory. Thus you are guaranteed of retrieval when *any* of these cues come to mind in the future. If you doubt this, think of how many times an unexpected retrieval cue (something you saw, heard, or thought) instantly reminded you of something you experienced years ago.

In recent years, the experiments of a Yale psychology professor, Endel Tulving, have contributed new knowledge concerning memory. According to Tulving's findings, we really don't forget things that we once learned. Instead we experience retrieval failure because we have difficulty finding the right retrieval cues to locate and release hidden information that, though still in memory, remains inaccessible.

By investing a few extra moments to provide your mind with meaningful retrieval cues about important items you are putting away, you are providing yourself with the means to recall this exact information at a future time. This method will work for you, especially if you expect it to work.

2. The Direct Access Retrieval Technique (DART)

In a previous section you worked with the cue-and-response idea in which you deliberately associated or linked two unrelated objects in your mind and then successfully recalled them later on. Remember the meatball and envelope? piano and fire?

0-98 and polka? pussycat and corporation? Once you created a vivid mental picture of interaction between any two of these items, each became a powerful retrieval cue for the other, and remembering them all was easy.

If you hadn't used vivid mental imagery to connect meatball with envelope, I could have given you the cue *meatball* all day, and it never would have retrieved the word *envelope.* But since it was the *right* retrieval cue for the word "envelope," it provided *direct access* to the word *envelope.* The cue *meatball* instantly located *envelope* and made it spring to the surface of your mind. It is as though you threw a "memory dart," and hit the *bull's eye* of recall. This is why I have named this the Direct Access Retrieval Technique (DART).

From this point on, much of this book will be devoted to teaching you how to create and work effectively with various kinds of direct access retrieval cues. Instead of talking to yourself, as in the previous method, you will now picture the object itself interacting vividly with the place in which it is put. The more vivid the imagery, the easier it will be to retrieve any item so stored. How do you make your mental pictures sufficiently vivid? By making each one as unusual or memorable as you can. Fill them with action! Make them funny or exaggerate them in some way. You can make them violent or erotic if you wish. Use any type of mental picture that is effective.

A little while ago, I casually mentioned a list of ten items and where they were put. Remember? This list included a ruler, a shopping list, a pair of glasses, a briefcase, dollar bills, a wristwatch, scissors, a letter, a deck of cards, and a book. In this exercise we will use the same list of items and locations. But this time you'll be using a direct access technique to register, retain, and retrieve them.

I will tell you how to picture some of the items and their locations; the rest will be up to you. It's important to realize that the pictures and associations you think of *yourself* are the ones that will work best. Even a single moment of thinking and picturing exerts a powerful force on your ability to remember. In fact, *it is this momentary effort itself that does the trick.*

HOW TO REMEMBER WHERE YOU PUT
TEN DIFFERENT ITEMS

The first item is your wristwatch, and you are putting it down on your kitchen table. Right now, in your mind's eye, see yourself accidentally *dropping* your watch onto the kitchen table. There goes the crystal! See it pop out, land on its edge, revolve and flip-flop in a circular motion, like a coin, on the tabletop. See it and hear it as it comes to rest next to the watch on the table. Now take an extra moment to see and hear this action picture in your mind's eye and ear before you go on. *Watch* and *kitchen table*.

Later on, when I ask you where you put the watch, just think of that wristwatch, what happened to it, and where. The very word *wristwatch* will cue and remind you of your popped out crystal, how it happened, and where. You should have no difficulty in answering, "On the kitchen table," as long as you have carefully followed the instructions. Rather than making a written notation of where you put something, you are literally writing it in your mind. You are, in other words, controlling your mental input so that you can dependably induce the mental output later on.

Now we're going to move more quickly, so be sure to read carefully and make effective and clear mental images for each item and its location. The next item is a ruler, which you place on the piano. *Ruler* and *piano*. See yourself taking a piano lesson: Your strict teacher strikes your knuckles with a ruler every time you make a mistake. Feel the pain *now* as you make another mistake and get a crack with the ruler.

If you ever *did* experience a situation like this, wouldn't it be hard to forget it? Therefore, why not deliberately contrive such a situation for the purpose of remembering? It's just a little creative common sense applied to memory. So before you go on, see it, hear it, and *feel it* as you take that painful piano lesson.

The next item is a pair of scissors, and you are putting it down on a chair. *Scissors* and *chair*. But don't just put it there; make it more dramatic: Take that scissors and stab the seat of the chair! See it stuck in the seat, vibrating back and forth. If you can see this, even for a moment, you'll have no difficulty remembering where that pair of scissors is later on. Scissors on the chair—see it now.

The next item is a shopping list, which you are putting on the gas range. Let's do this one quickly. See yourself placing the shopping list on the gas range, but as you do so, the flame from a burner ignites the paper, and your shopping list burns up in a blaze of glory. *Shopping list—gas range.* Take a moment to see the action clearly.

The next item is a pair of glasses. You are putting them on the sink. See some action! Just as you put the glasses down on the sink, a dish falls from an overhead cabinet and lands on your glasses, shattering the lenses all over the sink. See it and hear it now. A moment is all it takes. See it clearly: *glasses—sink.*

All of this, of course, has to do with the first of the 3 R's of Remembering—*registration.* With these mental pictures, you are learning the material in the first place so that you can recall it later at will. Through vivid registration of each item and its location, you will be able to retain and retrieve them successfully. Information well registered is information well remembered.

Before we continue, let's do a quick review. I'll give you the name of each item that you put someplace, and as I do so, let each such item bring back the mental picture you made. You will then know exactly where each item was put.

1. Where did you put the *wristwatch?*
2. Where did you put the *ruler?*
3. Where is the pair of *scissors?*
4. Where is the *shopping list?*
5. Where did you put the *glasses?*

I would be surprised if you didn't remember the answers quickly and correctly. Now, let's continue.

The next item is a letter, which you are putting on your bed. One of my seminar participants associated letter and bed with the thought *love letter*. That was all he needed to remember that the letter was on the bed. Many times an apt thought or phrase by itself, with no mental picture, will do the trick. Why not try it now? Just remember that that letter was a love letter, so you put it on the bed.

The next item is dollar bills, which you are placing on the dryer. Now, how in the world can you connect dollar bills with a dryer? Just use a little imagination. Suppose you just finished making these bills yourself (the master counterfeiter), and the money is still wet. See yourself putting those wet bills on the dryer. Or, if you prefer, take a moment to create your own mental picture. Do it now, before you go on. Just a moment or two is long enough, but make it vivid. *Dollar bills* and *dryer*.

The next item is a deck of cards, and you put it on the television. See some action on the TV screen involving a magician, gambling, or whatever strikes your fancy. It's up to you, so make your mental picture now. *Cards* and *television*.

The next object is a book, and you put it on top of the typewriter. Take your time in making the connections. *Book* and *typewriter*.

The last item is your briefcase, which you put in the closet. Maybe you want to hide it there because of what's inside that briefcase—who knows? Make the placement now, with your own thoughts and picture. *Briefcase* and *closet*.

That completes the list of ten items and ten locations. It's unlikely that you would have to use this technique ten times in one day to remember where you put ten things. The problem of trying to recall where you put something may not come up more than once or twice in any given day. But there is a reason for doing this exercise ten times with ten locations, as you just did. I'll name the reason in a few moments.

First, let's try this final quiz to see how well you can recall where you put each of the ten items we worked with. Again, I'll give you the cue (the item itself). Your job is to come up with the correct place in which each of the items was put. (The correct answers will be given later.)

To make things a bit more interesting, I'll list the ten items in scrambled order. I may even give you the location of an item as a cue, and ask you to recall which item was put there. Don't hurry; devote as much time as you need to each of the following items.

1. Where are the dollar bills?
2. Where is the briefcase?
3. Where did you put your glasses?
4. Where did you put the shopping list?
5. Where is the ruler?
6. Where is the book?
7. Where did you put the deck of cards?
8. Where is the letter?
9. Where is the wristwatch?
10. Where did you put the scissors?

Now reverse the process for variety. I'll name each of the locations. See if you can recall the particular item put there.

1. What did you put in the closet?
2. What did you put on the gas range?
3. What was put on the typewriter?
4. What was put on the bed?
5. What is on the chair?
6. What is on the dryer?
7. What did you put on the sink?
8. What is on the kitchen table?
9. What was put on the television set?
10. What did you put on the piano?

The correct answers to the first ten questions follow:

1. on the dryer
2. in the closet
3. on the sink
4. on the gas range

5. on the piano
6. on the typewriter
7. on the television set
8. on the bed
9. on the table
10. on the chair.

The correct answers for the second set of ten questions are:

1. the briefcase
2. the shopping list
3. the book
4. the letter
5. the scissors
6. the dollar bills
7. the glasses
8. the wristwatch
9. the deck of cards
10. the ruler

No doubt, you did very well in remembering these items and their locations. If you actively followed the instructions, you should have had no trouble at all. You now have two powerful methods you can use anytime, to quickly and dependably remind you of where you put things and to save you the time it could take to look for them. All you have to do is to remember to use these methods when you need them.

A little while ago I said that there was a reason for doing this memory exercise with ten different items, even though you probably wouldn't use the technique more than once or twice in any given day. Actually, that's part of the reason. Now that you know from your own experience that you have successfully used this method to help you remember where you put *ten* different items, then certainly remembering only one or two items will be child's play. You should now feel confident in and positive about this useful new memory skill.

You have been associating or linking things in your mind and forming mental images all your life, whether or not you are aware of it. All of your reading, your thinking and learning, your daily experiences, are filled with constant associations and mental imagery. When you last read a good story, the fact that you could imagine it and see it in your mind's eye as you read is what enabled you to understand and enjoy it. Reading is not learning; *imaging* is learning.

In the previous exercises you used these very same natural powers of picturing and associating to learn and remember specific things. But you have *deliberately, consciously* used this power. You should realize by now that in these exercises you have quite literally been in control of your own memory process of registration, retention, and retrieval. You have controlled both the input and the output of your memory through the application of direct access Memory Control technique. In short, by so doing, you have *made* your memory work for you.

SUMMARY

In this chapter you have learned two practical methods for remembering where you put things. The first, the talking technique, is useful for either temporary or long-term remembering. For one or two items and their locations that you want to recall later in the same day, simply use the method as it was originally explained. For longer-term recall, reinforce your registration with William James's Multiple Association Technique, as taught.

The second method, using mental picturing, is intended primarily for short-term recall of where you put things on a day-to-day basis. The mental pictures you make may last days or fade within hours, depending on the vividness of your original pictorial registrations.

Remember our first memory exercise, the Brain Chain? With this sequential linking technique, you memorized and recalled a list of twelve different items, in correct order, forward and backward. Then, in another exercise, using the cue-and-response technique, you deliberately registered and remembered six different words and their six unrelated associate words. And in our last exercise, designed for remembering where you put things, you registered retrieval cues and their locations, giving you direct access to the recall of ten items and ten places.

You might find it interesting to know that when you add all these items up, they represent a total of *forty-four things successfully learned and remembered.* (Minus, perhaps, a few that you might have missed.) But even if your successful retrieval total is, say, 39 or 40 items, this is still very good, especially when compared to the much lower total you would have scored without the use of these specialized memory techniques.

In view of your success so far with these principles and techniques, can it be said that you have improved your natural, inborn, innate memory capacity? Not necessarily. But it *can* be said that you have measurably improved the *performance* of your memory. And from a practical, realistic standpoint, that's all that counts.

6

The Secret of
Making Things
Easy to Remember

Up to this point you have been learning how to remember things that are normally difficult for most people to remember: groups of unrelated words, lists of items, telephone and other numbers of various types, and the exact locations of many specific items. These, plus other things such as names and faces, speech material, facts, and printed materials, are only a few of the kinds of information people have trouble remembering.

On the other hand, there are also many things that are very easy to remember, things that hardly anyone has trouble with. In fact, these things are so easy for people to remember that they don't even have to try. Such information just seems to be there when you need it. Examples include personal information about yourself, your spouse, your children, or others who are close to you; their names, their ages, their likes and dislikes. It could be information about your job or profession that is so familiar and secure that remembering it is effortless and automatic.

Many kinds of information, besides personal or work-related information, are just as easy to remember. The question I'm leading to is: *Exactly what is it that makes some things easier to remember than others?* To put it another way, what is it that makes those "easy" things so easy to remember?

Once you understand what makes such things so easy to remember, you can begin to extract this essense from them and apply it to the specific things that are difficult for you to remember. Thus, these difficult things become far easier for you to register, retain, and recall.

THE *FLO* OF MEMORY

There are three categories of things that we all remember without memory aids of any kind:

1. things you think about, or do, *frequently*
2. things that are *linked* (or associated) with each other
3. things that are *outstanding* in your mind

The first letters of the words, *Frequency, Link*, and *Outstanding* form the acronym *FLO*.

Category 1: Things You Think About, or Do, *Frequently*

Whatever type of work you do, you remember how to do because of frequent or repeated training you received in the past and/or frequent performance in the present. You do your work because you remember how, and you remember how because you do it. The key memory element here is *frequency*. It is no different for a concert pianist or tennis pro. They spend thousands of hours practicing and performing. As long as they use their skills in frequent practice or performance, they retain this mental and physical proficiency. If they take days, weeks, or months off, their skills diminish; they become rusty; their mind and muscles "forget." It is only by getting back into condition that they can recreate their former performance efficiency. The old saying, "Use it or lose it," is an ever-present fact of life. And memory is no exception.

Especially in memory, the frequent use of a fact, name, date, formula, speech, or entire body of knowledge still constitutes the best guarantee of effective retention and recall. Just thinking about something at various intervals is meaningful repetition. *Repetition is retention.* *Frequent* repetition is prolonged retention.

Category 2: Things That Are *Linked* or Associated with Each Other

If you think of your brain as a vast interlinking system, an immense associative network, then the concept of memory training is considerably clarified. The linking of a new fact, figure, or other material you want to remember to something you already know is the basis of all learning and remembering. Every new thing you learn is linked in some way to your previous knowledge, and when you can find the right cues to give to your mind, you can relink and retrieve the desired information again.

In previous memory exercises you consciously linked various items, after which merely thinking of one brought back the other. With the Brain Chain technique of linking, you were able to remember a string of twelve unrelated objects. One thing led to the other from beginning to end and from end to beginning! This was a dramatic example of the power and effectiveness of linking and the universal reminder principle.

Category 3: Things That Are *Outstanding* in Your Mind

Anything in your experience that is outstanding in some way or another is naturally easier to remember and therefore harder to forget. This could be almost anything that is unusual, exaggerated, painful, pleasurable, violent, colorful, full of action, dangerous, and so on. If you were sitting in a restaurant and a waiter suddenly, accidentally spilled hot soup over you, you would have little trouble remembering the event. You wouldn't have to take notes, study it, or review it in order to remember it, because it was so outstanding. Your brain would instantly register this event as an intense and traumatic experience that you would always remember. It is hardly necessary to point out that this experience would always remain outstanding in your memory.

It is in your power to create frequency merely by using or thinking about the specific information you want to remember. Indeed, you can do this at will. It is also in your power to deliberately link or associate things at will. And it is in your power to make anything you choose outstanding by picturing it as such or thinking of it in a way that is striking, vivid, or otherwise outstanding. If you could see Abraham Lincoln eating an ice cream cone, would you be able to forget it? Well, then, why not simply create that picture in your mind's eye? *See* it happening, and it will be memorable. Remember that your subconscious accepts as genuine whatever you see or visualize. It does not differentiate; it only remembers.

So, *frequency, linking*, and the *outstanding* are the three elements that form the natural FLO of memory.

THE MASTER PRINCIPLE OF MEMORY

When all is said and done, the thing your mind remembers best is *meaning*. This is the master principle of memory: The more meaning, the better the memory. The less meaning, the more difficult it is to remember. The mind must be able to detect meaning to work with. It is the very substance of memory, the raw material of your mind. Without meaning to process, there can hardly *be* anything to remember. At this moment, as you read these lines, your mind is forgetting the words, but it is busy extracting their meaning.

The FLO of Memory and Meaning

Anything you think about frequently intensifies its own meaning *because* of this frequency. Facts that are linked together create and intensify their own meaning *because* of that mental connection. And any name, fact, story, or other bit of knowledge that is somehow outstanding in your mind is all the more meaningful *because* it stands out. It is meaning that produces the memory imprint.

With these facts in mind, it is obvious that almost anything can be made easier to remember if it is made more meaningful. Through the years many memory aids based on the intensification of meaning have been created. In reality, they are mental holding devices that have stood the test of time.

MENTAL HOLDING DEVICES

A Selection of Mnemonic Devices (Memory Aids)

Broadly speaking, the following memory aids fall into three categories: first-letter mnemonics, rhymes, and striking phrases or mental pictures. Some of these mnemonics may be familiar to you.

First-Letter Mnemonics

Music. Do you remember the names of the four spaces between the lines on the treble clef music staff: They are F, A, C, and E. These letters form the acronym FACE. Music teachers capitalize on this coincidence and teach it as a memory aid to beginning music students. Perhaps you remember that the five lines of the music staff represent E, G, B, D, and F. If you do not, you still might remember the mnemonic sentence "*Every Good Boy Does Fine*," which creates meaning out of the meaningless sequence *E-G-B-D-F* and keeps these letter names in your mind. There is also an easy way to remember the four voices in a‑ choir—*Soprano, Tenor, Alto,* and *Bass.* Yes, the memory aid is the word STAB.

I was a music major in college, and I still remember the main periods in music history because of an acrostic sentence I composed at that time. These periods are, in order, *A*ntiquity, *P*olyphonic, *B*aroque, *C*lassical, *R*omantic, *M*odern, and *C*ontemporary. The mental holding device I created was this simple sentence: "*A*ll *P*eriods *B*ecome *C*lassified *R*egarding *M*ost *C*omposers." This sentence not only makes sense in itself, but it holds that information *in formation* for me whenever I need it.

I also recall the unusual acrostic I made up to remember the six ancient musical modes—*I*onian, *D*orian, *P*hyrigian, *L*ydian, *M*ixo-lydian, and *A*eolian. I merely took the first letter of each mode and formed the nonword IDPLMA. I pronounced it "ID-PLuMA," and I have remembered those six musical modes to this day.

Colors. The colors of the spectrum are red, orange, yellow, green, blue, indigo, and violet. A well-known acronym for this sequence is ROY G. BIV. An acrostic sentence that holds this information just as well is, "*R*ich *O*ld *Y*okels *G*et *B*igger *I*n *V*igor."

Astronomy. For remembering the planets in order, moving away from the sun—*M*ercury, *V*enus, *E*arth, *M*ars, *J*upiter, *S*aturn, *U*ranus, *N*eptune, *P*luto—just learn the following sentence: "*M*y *V*ery *E*legant *M*other *J*ust *S*erved *U*s *N*ine *P*izzas." You might even use the names of two imaginary people, such as M. VEM and J. SUNP.

Geography. To recall the names of the five Great Lakes—Huron, Ontario, Michigan, Erie, and Superior—just think of the word HOMES. To recall them from west to east, use this sentence: "*S*ergeant *M*ajor *H*ates *E*ating *O*nions." From east to west, a good sentence might be: "*O*strich *E*ggs *H*ave *M*etal *S*hells." (Untrue, but memorable!)

An easy aid to remembering that California, Oregon, and Washington are the only states on the west coast is the word COW. The only four states whose boundaries intersect at one point are Utah, Colorado, Arizona, and New Mexico. You can remember this with U = CAN. The acronym WISE brings to mind the four main divisions within the United Kingdom: *W*ales, *I*reland, *S*cotland, and *E*ngland.

Physics. The word PLAN brings to mind the formula for

engine horsepower: *P*ressure x *L*ength x *A*rea x *N*umber of revolutions.

Sales. A sales training reminder for salespeople to keep their presentation simple is the word KISS: "*K*eep *I*t *S*imple, *S*alespeople." To arouse your customer's *A*ttention, *I*nterest, *D*esire, and *A*ction, remember the opera title AIDA.

Real Estate. The word READS is a reminder of five benefits from investing in real estate: *R*eturn, *E*quity, *A*ppreciation, *D*epreciation, and *S*pendable income. Other acronyms would do just as well: DEARS, DARES, AS RED, OR SR. ADE.

Anatomy. The five layers of the scalp (*S*kin, *C*lose connective tissue, *A*poneurosis, *L*oose connective tissue, and *P*ericranium), neatly fit the word SCALP! There are many such memory aids to help medical students register, retain, and recall bodily structures.

Rhymes as Reminders

Remembering with rhymes is a highly efficient technique. The rhyme remembers! In Memory Control, a rhyme is to the ear what a picture is to the eye. I am sure that you will recognize the following memory-aid rhymes:

History. In fourteen hundred and ninety-two,
Columbus sailed the ocean blue.

The Calendar: Thirty days hath September,
April, June, and November. (etc.)

Spelling: "I before E
except after C
or when sounded as A
as in neighbor and weigh."

Other Reminders that Add Meaning for Memory

(Mental Pictures, Association, Striking Thoughts, Phrases)

Nautical. To remember that *port* is to the left, just think of the sentence, "The ship *left* port." To differentiate *bow* from stern, just remember that when you *bow*, you bend your body toward the *front*.

Nature. To remember the difference a stala*C*tite and a stala*G*mite, just remember that the C is for "ceiling" (stala*C*-tites hang from the *C*eiling) and the G is for *G*round (stala*G*mites come from the *G*round up).

Seasonal Time Change. To know whether to set the clock ahead or back one hour, just think of this well-known mnemonic: *"Spring forward, fall back."*

The Map. Could you recognize the outline of Turkey on an unmarked map? Or Bolivia? Most people can't. But could you recognize Italy on such a map? You would probably do so instantly, because you remember that Italy looks like a boot! Years ago you were taught to make this association. In this case, *boot* is a mental holding device for the information *Italy*. You connected these two thoughts many years ago, and it still works —such is the power of these reminders.

Setting the Table. My wife used to chide me because I put the fork on the wrong side of the plate when I helped set the table. I would always place the fork on the right instead of the left side of the plate, until the word *forklift* occurred to me one day. I saw the connection right away, and I have never made that mistake again. (Forklift = fork left.)

Such ingenious little reminders can make a lot of difference. Some time ago I bought a small tape recorder that has one thumb-lever for all modes of operation. Because this was different from other recorders I used, I had trouble getting used to the fact that pushing that lever *down* would produce the playback mode. I thought about this little problem, and the word *downplay* popped into my mind. I have never had that problem since!

Shopping. Many times you can invent a quick mnemonic to remind you of items to buy at the supermarket. These aids come in very handy when you don't have a pencil and your list is short. For example, suppose you need bread, butter, oranges, and milk. Merely by mentally rearranging those items, you come up with *B*read, *O*ranges, *M*ilk, *B*utter, and you have the word BOMB. Later, when you shop, you just think of the acronym BOMB, decode it to retrieve the original items, and presto! Your shopping is done.

All of these simple mental holding devices or mnemonic devices help make forgettable information almost unforgettable. The presence of unusual or vivid meaning is what makes them work. Mnemonics can be *any* kind of aid that helps you remember better. No matter what you call them, all such aids are really retrieval cues. Anything that triggers your memory—a striking association, a pattern, a rhyme . . . to trigger remembering—is a retrieval cue. Because these cues have such significant power, we will harness as much of it as possible with the techniques of Memory Control.

SUMMARY

In this chapter we isolated the three things you remember most easily and naturally: things used or experienced *frequently*, things *linked* together, and things that are *outstanding* in some way. From here on, think of this as the natural FLO of memory. It is important to remember that it is entirely within your power to create frequency, link things together, and make things outstanding in your mind.

You are now ready to learn one of the most interesting and valuable lessons in Memory Control training: names and faces, or the art of remembering people.

7

A Working Memory
for Names and Faces

The most uncomplimentary thing you can say to anybody is, "I remember your face, but I can't remember your name." That simple statement of fact is a scathing slight in any language. You may as well come out and say, "I can't remember your name because you are not important enough for me to remember." It doesn't matter how you say it, because this is how it is *heard*, and no amount of explaining will change the effect of those ten little words.

Forgetting names not only causes momentary embarrassment; it can also cost you a new acquaintance, an associate, a client, a business opportunity, or even a potential friend. The name of the game in life is people, and the sweetest sound to most people's ears is still the sound of their own name.

There's an old saying: "Remember me and I'll never forget you; but forget me and I'll never forgive you." That says almost everything there is to say about the importance of remembering people's names.

When you get right down to it, the basic reason people don't remember names is that they don't pay attention. The time to learn a name properly is right away, when you first meet someone. Like most people, however, you are probably more interested in making a good impression rather than in letting the other person's name make a proper impression on you. Many times you probably feel that you will never see this new person again, "so why bother about the name?" When you *do* meet that same person a day, week, or month later, it is very embarrassing if you can't call him or her by name.

Since remembering people's names is so important, you might think that a subject like this would be taught in schools of business and communication. Unfortunately, it rarely is, and millions of people who can't remember names still walk around calling others, "Buddy," "Mac," "Fella," "Chief," "Governor," "Charlie," "Buster," "Doc," "Pal," "Chum," "Friend," "Young man," "Handsome," "Good-looking," "Honey,"· "Darling," "Lady," "Baby," "Beautiful," "Gorgeous," "Princess," or "Hey!" A memory defect for names is a communications defect.

Years ago, when it came to recalling names, my memory was like magic—it disappeared! Other people would shake hands and then forget a name five minutes after an introduction; I would forget the name while we were still shaking hands! Later, when I learned to do something about it, I realized that my forgetfulness with names had nothing to do with *forgetting*, but simply with *not getting* them in the first place.

TWO METHODS FOR REMEMBERING NAMES

I am going to teach you two methods for remembering people's names. Each method is complete in itself or can be used in combination with the other. The first one, the Salt System, is short, simple, and basic. It is based on common sense and simple repetition, and it requires very little effort. It is for people who want to improve their memory for names but who do not want to learn a more advanced or complete memory control technique.

The second method, which I call the C-C-R System (Convert-Connect-Review), requires more time to learn, but it is worth it if you really want to remember names and faces like a pro. If necessary, you could remember a banquet hall full of people with the CCR method; however, I recommend that you be practical and proficient, not incredible or phenomenal, unless you want to go into show business.

The SALT System

Years ago Samuel Johnson said that the true art of memory is the art of attention. This is still true. If you want to be able to remember names, you may as well make it easier for yourself by paying attention and getting the name right in the first place.

Remember the PAR formula: *P*ay *A*ttention and *R*emember.

If you register the name correctly, you will retain it; if you retain it, you can retrieve it. Everything in memory comes back to the importance of those three Rs of memory processing: registration, retention, and retrieval. Right now, we are dealing with the first of these three Rs, *registration*.

When you are meeting someone, if you do not hear the name clearly, or if, for any reason, you are not sure you got the name right, *don't wait*! Ask that person to repeat the name for you then and there. After the name is repeated, say the name aloud. For even better registration, ask the person to spell the name for you. Listen carefully, then spell the name again yourself. As you hear the person spell the name, and as you spell it yourself, mentally picture each successive letter and let the complete name form itself in your mind's eye. This simple spelling idea forces your mind to concentrate on the name, and clearer, sharper registration is attained.

The next step is to ask a conversational question, *using the name as part of the question*: "Are you from this area, Mr. Hannigan?" Then, during the conversation, be sure to use the name whenever it seems appropriate. Each of these successive repetitions hammers the name in deeper. Finally, be sure to say the name again at the end of the conversation: "It was nice to talk with you, Mr. Hannigan. Good-bye."

Can you see what has happened during this procedure? During the introduction alone you heard the name at least three times (instead of the usual *once*). You also heard the spelling of the name and used the name during conversation and again at the end of the conversation. You have heard the name, you have said the name, you have spelled the name, and you have heard it spelled by the other person. And, of course, during all of this, you have been seeing the person's face and features right in front of you. By this time your subconscious mind has had the opportunity to begin to connect the name with the face.

What I have just described is the SALT System for remembering people's names. I will now teach it to you in detail, step by step, so that you can apply it methodically and make what I described above happen every time you deliberately choose to remember a name.

SALT is an acronym to help you remember the following four steps so that you can use them at will:

S = *S*ay and *S*pell the name.
A = *A*sk a question, *using the name.*
L = *L*earn the name by repeating it appropriately during conversation.
T = *T*erminate the conversation by using the name once more.

You can easily memorize the four SALT steps by repeating the meaning of each of the letters in the acronym until you know them by heart. You *don't* have to memorize the exact wording given above. Just know the meaning of each letter and exactly what you are to do.

How to Use the SALT System

Here is an example of the SALT System in action:
"Hello, I'm Mort Herold."
"How do you do. I'm *Carol Borovic.*"

Say: "*Carol Borovic.* That's an interesting name. Can you spell it for me?"

Spell: "Sure. B-O-R-O-V-I-C, *Borovic.*"

"I see. B-O-R-O-V-I-C."

Ask: "Are you from this area, Ms. *Borovic?*"

Learn: Learn the name as you *use* it appropriately, during the conversation.

Terminate: "It was nice to talk to you, Ms. *Borovic.*"

There it is. With this simple formula you have heard the name five times in the first thirty seconds or less, plus its proper spelling twice. And remember, we haven't even included your use of the name during conversation. All of this is accomplished easily, in a relaxed, natural manner, always following the natural sequence of SALT.

Memory researchers have found that people remember names about 30 percent better when they repeat the other person's name at the time of introduction. So don't just say, "Nice to meet you." *Repeat* that name when you first hear it and as often as is natural and appropriate afterward. You might ask the derivation of the name or what type of work Ms. Borovic does, or any other questions that will make her and her name more interesting and meaningful to you. The SALT sequence simply gives you an organized procedure for listening and learning the name while your subconscious is forming its own connections between the name and the face. When you follow this procedure closely, you will find it difficult *not* to remember the name!

The SALT System is based on multisensory registration and simple repetition—brief, natural, meaningful repetition.

The SALT System is most effective in meeting relatively small numbers of people rather than large groups. There must be no rush or undue tension during the initial meeting and conversation. Just relax, *take your time with each person,* and you will learn those names.

For learning names of many people, the more advanced CCR System is the one to use. Even so, the SALT System is an integral part of the CCR System, as you will soon realize. The "say and spell" procedure of SALT is still the best method of originally hearing the name in the first place.

The CCR System

"I used to have trouble remembering names until I took the Sam Carnegie Course."

Anonymous

When all is said and done, the only way to learn and remember names and faces is *to control the process by which learning and remembering takes place*. This means control of registration, retention, and retrieval. The CCR System takes care of this in a systematic and reliable manner. You convert, connect, and review in the following manner:

- *Convert* the name and face into meaningful retrieval cues.
- *Connect* the name cue and face cue so that "one without the other" becomes a virtual psychological impossibility.
- *Review* these connections for secure retention and retrieval.

More specifically, this is accomplished in five steps:

	1. *Get the name clearly!* (Follow the first step, *S*, of the SALT System.)
CONVERT	**2.** Give the name meaning for your memory to grasp (the name cue).
	3. Pick a feature of the face that is striking or noticeable (the face cue).
CONNECT	**4.** Mentally associate the name cue with the face cue in a vivid way.
REVIEW	**5.** Reinforce these connections with adequate review.

We will now take each step at a time so that you can understand and apply them all properly.

Step 1: Get the Name Clearly.

Begin by following the first step, *S*, of the SALT System. Use steps A, L, and T when and if you can, but do not let them interfere with steps 2, 3, 4, and 5 of the CCR procedure. Again, hear the name and get it right in the first place.

Step 2: Give the Name Meaning (Forming the Name Cue).

In this step you try to recognize any obvious meaning the name may hold for you. If there is some meaning, it will be easy to mentally picture the name and connect it to the face. If there is no recognizable meaning, convert the name into something that *is* meaningful to you.

Let's say that the name you hear is Pidgeon. Pidgeon has definite meaning; you can easily picture a pigeon poking about on the ground and use this picture as a perfect name cue to remind you later of the name.

Suppose the name you hear is Cotton. Here is another name whose meaning you instantly recognize. You can easily picture some fluffy, white, soft cotton balls. Mentally picturing such things in your mind's eye is a very important part of the technique, so please don't think that because cotton is so easily picturable you don't actually have to see it in your mind's eye as clearly as you can. You *do*, or you may not be able to remember that name!

Here is another name: Radke (pronounced Rad-kee). Now this one does not have any immediately recognizable meaning, as did Pidgeon and Cotton. So, at the moment it may seem a bit more difficult to create a retrieval cue. This is where the Conversion technique comes into play; you convert a name without meaning into a name *with* meaning. This name conversion works exactly like the Number-Meaning Method you learned in Chapter 4. You learned how to change (convert) numbers without meaning into numbers with meaning. This new meaning not only reminded you of the number, but it decoded itself into the original number as well. You can do the same thing, in the same way, with "meaningless" names. You convert them into some other word or phrase that sounds like the original name and/or that has meaning, and that can be pictured. Let's go back to the name Radke.

What other word or words sound like Rad-kee? How about Rat-Key or Red-Key? It's easy to picture a rat with a key in its mouth, isn't it? The fact that it is very unlikely for a rat to have a key in its mouth makes it all the more memorable, especially if you visualize it. Even the simple phrase *red key* has meaning; it *sounds* like Radke, and it can easily be visualized.

Remember that your memory is an association machine that operates on reminders, whether you call them cues, retrieval cues, or name cues. *One thing reminds you of another.* This is the universal law of all remembering. What we are doing here is simply helping nature along by providing such reminder cues. These reminders are words that sound like the name, plus mental pictures to intensify the impression, so that later recall will be easy and reliable. Take the name Mahoney. Unless you know someone by that name, *Mahoney* means very little by itself. But you can think of it as *my honey* and see your spouse or sweetheart. But if you rhyme it with *baloney*, you suddenly have something you can not only see, but also touch, taste, and even smell. A powerful group of reminders indeed, for your mind's eye, ear, and other senses!

Try the name Buckley. Does it have any meaning for you? If not, you might think of someone you know named Bucky. If you do, *see* him in your mind's eye; Bucky is then your name cue. If not, what about the word *Buckle*? It doesn't rhyme, but that's not really necessary. Remember, all you need is a reminder. And *buckle* is close enough to *Buckley* to bring that name to mind. You could even use *bucket* or *bug-free*, or whatever else reminds you of Buckley. See the action in your mind's eye, and you'll have all the meaning you need to retrieve the original name.

Three Types of Names and How and When to Convert Them. Broadly speaking, there are three categories of names:

1. names with obvious meaning
2. names without obvious meaning, but which still remind you of something (reminder names)
3. names with no meaning (blanks)

The names in the first category are the easiest and quickest to work with and convert to mental pictures. The names *Pidgeon* and *Cotton* are in this category. You don't have to look for or create meaning for them. The name itself *is* the meaning. Other such names would be Fox, Baker, Moon, Glass, Forest, Walker, Gold, Melon, Herring, Coyne, Nutt, Winters, Sommer, Taylor, Star, Berry, Blackstone, White, Waters, Shepherd, Flowers, and so forth.

The second category of names includes those without much specific meaning but which still can remind you of something. For example, the name Campbell has no clear meaning, but it can easily remind you of soup! Or the name Carter might remind you of Jimmy Carter, Carter's liver pills, or Carter's ink, among others.

Another name, Serta, most likely brings to your mind the word *mattress*. Reminder names can remind us of a person we know, a celebrity, a product, a place, a book, a title, almost anything. A name like Davis, for instance, can bring to mind the Davis Cup in tennis, Sammy Davis, Jr., or Avis (car rental), or a woman you know named Mavis (rhymes). Carver can remind you of a knife. Rosenblum can bring to mind the phrase *rose in bloom* or *rose and plum*. The name Keaton might remind you of *kitten*, Diane Keaton, or Buster Keaton. I'm sure you get the idea. The name reminds you of a name cue, and the name cue reminds you of the name.

Finally, we come to names with no meaning. This category is the largest of all three. If you look at any phone book, you will soon see that the vast majority of names have no meaning. It is in this category that the conversion technique shines. In the 1800s, an American mnemonist, Pliny Miles, first used this idea, which he called assimilation.

Here are some examples of no-meaning (or blank) names: Mykowski, Okimoto, Siegel, Silvestri, Kringer, Moschino, Smeltzer, Esposito, Papanicoladu, and Monticello.

When you first hear it, the name Mykowski, for instance, may seem like a perfect blank as far as meaning is concerned. But if you just separate the syllables in Mykowski, you have My-kow-ski, which instantly converts to "*My cow skis.*" With this simple process you have converted the meaningless name *Mykowski* into a phrase *with* meaning. Incidentally, have you ever seen a cow ski? If you did, you would never forget it. It would be so outstanding in your mind that nothing could erase the memory. By converting Mykowski into "My cow skis" (and mentally picturing a cow skiing), you have *created* that unforgettable improbability for your mind to register, and you have a name cue for Mykowski.

Dividing names into syllables is one good way to invent meaningful name cues. Other ways are equally effective. Take the name *Okimoto*, for example. The sound of that name could remind you of *locomotive*, or *O-K Photo*, because they are relatively similar in sound to the name *Okimoto*.

Take the name *Siegel*: Using the similar sound idea, Siegel easily converts to *sea gull* or "*see a girl.*" Or, even better in this case, Siegel rhymes with *beagle* (picture the dog), *regal* (picture a queen's crown, etc.), and *legal* (picture a lawyer or judge).

With the similar sound or rhyme technique, the name *Kringer* could easily convert to *stinger* (the drink or a bee), or singer, finger, Klinger (if you know someone by that name), or ringer (picture a ring or bell ringing).

In the same way the name *Smeltzer* could become *seltzer*. Suppose you met a person named Silvestri. Look for a similar sound, and you get *silver strings* or *"see the best tree."* For Moschino, use a *cherry* (maraschino cherry); for Esposito, use *"Expose a toe."* Remember, the sounds do not have to be exact rhymes, just similar. All you need is a reminder.

Many times the syllable idea is best for converting longer names into name cues. The name Papanicoladu, for example, becomes *"Papa's nickle on you."* The name Monticello converts into *Monty's cello, mound o'jello, mounty fellow, mountain yellow, want a fellow, Monty bellows, "Monty, hello!," county fellow, Auntie Bella,* or *Mountain Gallo* (the California wine).

It is important to realize that any name can be made meaningful (and usually picturable) with the Name Conversion Technique. Lots of names have many possibilities (the name Monticello, for example). The answers (name cues) are in the names themselves. All you have to do is find them. Yes, it takes attention, observation, and imagination. Any worthwhile skill requires some effort; but, remember that this kind of effort is creative, enjoyable, progressively easier, and valuable. The result is that you remember names!

In the beginning of this chapter I said that the basic reason people have trouble remembering names is lack of attention. One of the beauties of applying the Conversion Technique is that it forces you (without your being aware of it) to pay close attention to the name in order to convert it into a name cue. You *must* concentrate in order to do this. There is no other way to come up with a workable name cue.

The purpose of the Conversion Technique is not only to give names more meaning, but to *see* them as well as you see the face. When you meet someone you see the face but only *hear* the name, and usually you hear it only once. You remember best what you *see* rather than hear. That is why you recognize faces better and more quickly than you remember names.

Unless you use a method to hold the name for you, how long can you hang on to it? If you have ever run into someone whose face you recognize but whose name you can't remember, it is almost surely because your original registration of the name was so weak as to be nonexistent in comparison to the registration, by repeated sight, of the face.

Now you know why it is so important to convert names into name cues, preferably those that can easily be pictured. Such a name cue works as a powerful reminder of the name itself.

Forming these mental pictures is as close as we can come to seeing the name as well as seeing the face. The whole idea, of course, is to make it as easy to *remember* the name as it is to *recognize* the face.

To review, if the name you hear already has meaning you can recognize (like the names Lamb and Diamond), you simply mentally picture a lamb or a diamond. After you learn how to make the face remind you of your mental picture for the name, you will instantly recall the name when you see the face.

On the other hand, if the name you hear has no recognizable meaning, then you use the Conversion Technique. You think of something that sounds as much as possible like that name, and which does have picturable meaning, as in our previous examples. Usually, the first name cue you think of is the best one to use, because it is what you will think of first at a later time as well. The associative connection between the name and its name cue is so close that one will automatically remind you of the other. As a matter of fact, if you follow this procedure exactly as explained, there is no way that you can stop this from happening. This is what I meant before when I said that thinking of one without the other becomes a virtual psychological impossibility.

Such is the power of meaning, association, and mental picturing; just as the name cue recalls the name for you, so will the face recall the face cue, the name cue, and the name itself, in rapid order. Before we proceed to the technique for connecting the name cue with the face cue, we need more practice with names and name cues.

Review of Names and Name Cues. In the following list are some names we have already used as examples. Each one appears with a name cue to its right, with the type of cue it is listed at the far right. You are going to take a brief quiz in a moment or two, so *carefully* note each name and its name cue. Be sure you understand the association between each name and its cue.

The Name	Name Cue	Conversion Technique Used
RADKE	rat and key	Separate Syllables
MAHONEY	baloney	Rhyme
BUCKLEY	buckle	Similar Sound
CAMPBELL	soup	Reminder Name
CARTER	Jimmy Carter	Reminder Name
SIMMONS	mattress	Reminder Name
DAVIS	Sammy Davis, Jr.	Reminder Name
CARVER	knife	Reminder Name
ROSENBLUM	rose in bloom	Reminder Name
KEATON	kitten	Reminder Name
MYKOWSKI	my cow skis	Separate Syllables
OKIMOTO	locomotive	Similar Sound
SIEGEL	sea gull	Similar Sound
SILVESTRI	silver strings	Similar Sound
KRINGER	stringer	Rhyme
MOSCHINO	maraschino cherry	Reminder Name
SMELTZER	seltzer	Rhyme
ESPOSITO	expose a toe	Separate Syllables
PAPANICOLADU	Papa's nickel on you	Separate Syllables
MONTICELLO	mound o' jello	Separate Syllables

The following are name cues from the preceding list. Look at each cue and let it recall to your mind the original name. Do not look at the answers above. See how many of the original names you can retrieve from these name cues:

Name Cues	Write in the Name
Papa's nickel on you	_____
seltzer	_____
stringer	_____
sea gull	_____
my cow skis	_____
rose in bloom	_____
Sammy Davis, Jr.	_____
Jimmy Carter	_____
buckle	_____
rat and key	_____
mound o' jello	_____
expose a toe	_____
maraschino cherry	_____
silver strings	_____
locomotive	_____
kitten	_____
knife	_____
mattress	_____
soup	_____
baloney	_____

Now that you have the idea, it is time to do some name conversions on your own. Here is the exact method, reduced to two steps:

1. When you first hear a name, see if you recognize meaning in it. It may have obvious meaning, or it may remind you of something. If either case exists, make a mental picture of it. This will be your name cue.

2. If you recognize no meaning in the name itself, create meaning for the name with one of the following techniques:
   a. Similar sound, or rhyme
   b. Separate Syllables

You can always remember steps one and two through the following mnemonics:

1. The ROAM formula: *Recognize Or Add Meaning.*
2. The SRS formula: *Similar Sound/Rhyme/Separate Syllables.*

The following is a list of names for you to convert into name cues. As you look at each one, mentally ROAM around it to see if it is a meaning name, reminder name, or blank. Apply the SRS formula, where appropriate, to help you form the cues. If any of the names temporarily stump you, skip them and go on. You can return to them later. The best name cues are words or *short* phrases you can picture in your mind's eye.

Remember that a name cue does *not* have to have all the true sounds of the original name. Just include the main sounds, and the reminder will work. Your own memory will fill in the rest. Trust it.

Write your name cues in the space to the right of each name. One for each is enough. (Some possible Name-Cues for these names will be found on pages 236-237. Do not turn to that page until you are finished creating your own name cues.)

Name	Name-Cue
Ashkanazy	
Peilet	
Gotteson	
Klowden	
Meiners	
Wideikis	
Busch	
Rupchik	
Wrigley	
Hirschberg	
Robin	
Witherspoon	
Koronowski	
Endicott	
Grieg	
Byrne	
Kuehl	
Laflin	
Ott	
La Banco	

Step 3: Pick a Striking Facial Feature.

Face registration is comparatively simple, as was explained in detail earlier. Even if you don't look at a face continuously as you converse with a new acquaintance, the fact that you see the face even for a moment or two is usually enough to register it. Psychologists have repeatedly proven how well we remember things we have seen—even for a very short time. The old proverb, "One picture is worth a thousand words," is truer than you might think. Suffice to say that we remember faces without much trouble. Unfortunately, this fact doesn't do us much good as far as the name is concerned, unless we find something on that face to which we can connect the name cue.

You *convert* the name and *connect* it to the face. It is for this reason that you must observe the face carefully to find a feature that serves this purpose. You have already learned that all names either have built-in meaning or have no visible meaning, in which case *you* have to supply one. The situation is basically the same with faces. As you observe the face, either you notice some particular feature right away or you have to look and find one. When you find it, this becomes your *face cue*.

After you get your first impression of the whole face, begin to look for some feature that seems most noticeable or outstanding. The one that strikes you *first* is the best one to use as a face cue, because this is the first feature you will notice later on when you meet the person again. This feature might be thick lips, a high forehead, a widow's peak, a big nose, a crooked nose, a bald scalp, peculiar ears, a chin cleft, a dimple, a wart, a scar, a blemish, even or crooked teeth, white or yellow teeth, obvious bridgework, bushy eyebrows, big eyes, small eyes, wide-set eyes, a pointed chin, a square jaw, high cheekbones, flared nostrils, piercing eyes, sunken eyes, a clear complexion, discolored skin, or many others.

When you can't seem to find anything particularly noticeable or outstanding, just focus arbitrarily on some facial feature and exaggerate it in your mind's eye. Many times I have used the same face cue for many different people during the same evening. *It still works.*

Step 4: Associate the Name Cue with the Face Cue.

Step 4, the *connection*, locks name and face together in such a way that thinking of one without the other becomes psychologically impossible. If you form your retrieval cues correctly and connect them effectively, you will have set in motion a powerful, associative cause and effect that is virtually guaranteed to work.

Do you remember how well this technique worked earlier, when you learned to remember where you put ten different items? Instead of names and faces, you did it with items and locations. These twenty items were mentally put in different places, after which you were able to recall the *exact* location of each one. If you were given the name of the item, its location instantly flashed to your mind. In reverse, when I gave you each item's location, the name of each item popped into your mind. Each was a direct access retrieval cue for the other, and there was no way you could have stopped this powerful recall mechanism—unless you didn't follow directions, didn't pay attention, or didn't do the exercise.

MEETING TEN PEOPLE

At this point you are ready to begin one of the most interesting and valuable sections of this book. You will actually go through the step-by-step process of meeting ten new people and remembering their names!

From this point on it will be necessary for you to use your imagination to picture clearly and vividly every step of the way, exactly as I ask. The first name or two may be familiar to you. You learned previously how to convert them into name cues, but you did not learn to connect them to actual faces. The rest of the names are completely new. I will help you with some of them; the rest will be up to you.

The first person you meet is a Mr. Buckley. Please say the name to yourself and spell it. Do it now.

Although the name Buckley is meaningless, it reminds you of the word *buckle*. Visualize it now as a gold, shiny belt buckle with a big, bold letter *B* for Buckley on it. You must see it as clearly as you can. You now have the name cue, belt-buckle, and you can see the *B* for Buckley.

Now for the face: As you observe Mr. Buckley's face, the first thing you notice is his high forehead, which is also shiny. So use that high forehead as a face cue. To connect the gold belt buckle with the high forehead; see a belt around Mr. Buckley's head with the shiny gold buckle (with its letter *B*) right in the middle of his high forehead! See it clearly in your mind's eye as you look at him. Just seeing it like this for a moment or two is all that is necessary. Think of it now as Buckley's belt buckle with a *B*. Or *B* for Buckley's belt buckle, or use any unusual idea to verbally reinforce the connection in your mind. Once more really see Buckley with that shiny gold belt buckle on his forehead. Imagine him walking around like that!

Later, when you see Mr. Buckley again, you will notice his high forehead, and on it will be that shiny gold belt buckle, which will remind you of the name Buckley. All you will need are those reminders. Good-bye for now, Mr. Buckley.

The next person you meet is Mr. Okimoto. Get that name right—Okimoto. Spell it to yourself and picture the name in capital letters as you do so. The only word you can think of at the moment that sounds like Okimoto is locomotive. Use it as the name cue. You have noticed that Mr. Okimoto has thick, bushy eyebrows, which will serve nicely as a face cue. Now, to connect the locomotive with his bushy eyebrows, mentally picture a miniature locomotive steaming slowly out of his bushy left eyebrow toward the right eyebrow as it passes over the bridge of his nose. See the slow, steaming locomotive enter and then disappear into his bushy right eyebrow as its steam whistle suddenly blows. Hear it—and see the action—from left eyebrow to right. You might even think of the phrase, *"Okimoto's locomotive* steam, whistles, and raises *eyebrows."* See that action picture now once more and repeat that sentence to yourself to reinforce the action. (Later on, when you see him again, those bushy eyebrows will produce a little locomotive and, in turn, the name Okimoto.) Now, say to yourself, "Good-bye, Mr. Okimoto."

The next person you meet is Miss Siegel. Hear that name correctly—Siegel. S-I-E-G-E-L. Siegel sounds like sea gull. Good; you now have the name cue—sea gull. Now look carefully at Miss Siegel's face. You notice nothing especially prominent at first. Then you do notice her wide, flaring nostrils. The tip of her nose points upward slightly, and her sizable nostrils are easy to see, so you now exaggerate and enlarge them as the face cue. Supersized nostrils! Now, to connect sea gull to nostrils: See Miss Siegel sneezing through those super nostrils; as she sneezes, *hundreds* of noisily flapping sea gulls fly out of those nostrils! See it now; imagine a sight like that. How could one ever forget it? Noisy, flapping sea gulls continuously come from those big nostrils. Siegel's nostrils. See her sneeze again and watch the action. Hear those flapping wings. Siegel's sea gulls! Say good-bye to Miss Siegel.

These first three mental pictures and word associations have graphically shown exactly how your thinking and picturing process should take place in forming and connecting your name and face cues.

The idea is to make your mental pictures as unusual and extraordinary as you can. The usual and ordinary are forgotten first. The unusual and extraordinary are long remembered *because* they are so. Specifically, the name cue and the face cue should interact with one another in some kind of unusual action: locomotives traveling through eyebrows, shiny belt buckles banded around a head, or flapping sea gulls flying out of someone's nostrils.

Occasionally people complain that they were taught to think logically and that such bizarre or ridiculous mental picturing "goes against the grain" or is difficult in some way for them. The answer is, of course, not to use it if, after giving fanciful mental picturing a good try, you are still uncomfortable with it. Either bizarre or plausible imagery will work. Again, use whatever works for you; the only important factor is to make each picture vivid and full of action.

Before we meet more people, look at the formula below, which will help you create good, clear, result-producing mental pictures. I call it the USA formula. Basically, it stands for the *U*nusual: *S*ee it in *A*ction!

U = the *U*nusual, the outstanding (either bizarre or plausible).

S = *S*ee it (and hear it) *vividly* in your mind's eye and ear. Take a few seconds to do it right.

A = *A*ction! Active interaction between the name cue and face cue.

This A for action is very important. By *active interaction* I mean action that takes place specifically between the name and face cues. They must interact in some memorable way. Making them interact strengthens the connection. For example, instead of picturing an electric saw sitting next to a tree, you should see it *attacking* that tree and cutting right through the trunk! You must make this image vivid, as though it were happening in detail right there in front of you. *Hear* the saw buzzing as it eats through the tree. See that sawdust fly!

Perhaps now you can better appreciate Mr. OKIMOTO with his steaming "EYEBROW-LOCOMOTIVE," Mr. BUCKLEY with his shiny golden "FOREHEAD-BUCKLE," and Miss SIEGEL with her flaring "NOSTRILS and flapping SEA GULLS."

Now you are ready to meet Miss Wideikis. Spell the name to get it right. At the moment the name does not remind you of anything, even though you mentally ROAM around it. In this case your best bet is to apply the SRS formula to add meaning to the name (*S*imilar sound, *R*hyme, or *S*eparate syllables). We'll presume for the moment that you can't come up with a similar-sounding word or a rhyme for the name *Wideikis*. Next is the separate syllable method, and you come up with WID' A KISS —and there's your name cue. Again, it's a good idea to use the first usable cue you think of, because later this is usually the one you'll think of first again. At the moment, WID' A KISS may seem difficult to picture; but you can still use it as a word or thought association and connect it to a facial feature that is easily pictured. As you look at Miss Wideikis's face you note two or three possibilities: her long eyelashes, full lips, and strong chin. FULL LIPS—WID' A KISS! You now have your name and face cues. Mentally zero in on her full lips and exaggerate them until they are double their present size. Think to yourself, "superbig red lips, ready to kiss everything in sight!" As you look at those lips you see them kissing everything in sight, including you! There she is—WIDEIKIS, WID' A KISS; WIDEIKIS, WID' A KISS. Repeat it to yourself, see it, hear the juicy "smacks." See everything getting full of red lipstick, including your cheeks and shirt or blouse collar. By this time you are glad to say, "Good-bye, Miss Wideikis."

Next, you meet Mr. Mahler. Be sure to spell it and get it right. You decide to rhyme it with dollar, a good, workable name cue, MAHLER-DOLLAR. Mr. Mahler has big ears that protrude from his head, which become your face cue. *Dollar* and ears. As I write this, the word association "Ear's a dollar" (Here's a dollar) comes to mind. We'll try to use that to reinforce your mental picture. "Ears a dollar, in one ear and out the other"! Picture dollar bills going in one ear and out the other. It's a little bizarre but eminently picturable. So, right now, see Mr. Mahler's dollars, rolled up lengthwise, as he pushes them, one at a time, in one ear; then see them come out the other. See Mr. Mahler doing this right before your eyes, repeatedly. Hear him laughing loudly and jovially as he makes those dollar bills go in one ear and out the other. Good-bye, Mr. Mahler.

Next, you meet a Mr. Deiro. You're not sure you heard the name right, so you ask him to spell it for you, then you pronounce it again. He tells you Deiro is pronounced Darrow, "like arrow." Presto—you have your name cue, arrow. Now for the face: Look at him carefully; you spot a small but definite wart on his left cheek. Wart and arrow. See a long red arrow suddenly stuck in that wart. See it vibrating, having struck its mark. Later, when you bump into Mr. Deiro again, you'll notice the wart, which will remind you of the arrow, which will give you the name Deiro. Good-bye for now, Mr. Deiro.

You have just met six different people. You have converted their names, connected all name cues to face cues, and repeated these connections verbally and visually for initial reinforcement. In short, you have been applying the CCR System—convert, connect, review.

There are four final people to meet. One final tip before you continue: Remember to exaggerate or enlarge the facial feature you select. In this way whatever is already noticeable to you will become even more so. That's why we enlarged Miss Wideikis's lips and Miss Siegel's nostrils. From here on, you're on your own.

You are now meeting Ms. Peterson. She has a stunning smile, with perfect white teeth. Take whatever time you need to form your cues and connect them.

Next, you meet Mr. Nicholas. Mr. Nicholas has a dark moustache and a widow's peak. (Use either one.)

Next, you meet Miss Collins. Miss Collins is old but sprightly. She has many deep wrinkles in her face.

Last, you meet Mr. Charise. Mr. Charise has a deep cleft in his chin.

You have just met ten people, and you have applied the first two steps of the CCR sequence. You have converted and connected their names and faces. Now you are ready for the last step, review.

Step 5: Review Your Connections for Reinforcement

Reviewing your mental connections for each person is so important that I can hardly stress it enough. This final step, review, is what really does the trick. This review-reinforcement is what creates retention. When you meet people in groups, you do your reviewing after each three people you meet. You just walk to the side, look at those people you just met from the sidelines, and mentally re-form and review the mental picture connections you made for each person. Then you meet three more and keep repeating the process, reviewing your mental connections for each one.

At this point it is time to look around the room and review the people you have met in our exercise. I will help you to do this by mentioning each person's name, the selected facial feature, and the connection. Your job is to picture each of these people as vividly as you did before.

The Review. First, you met Mr. Buckley. See his high, shiny forehead. Right in the middle of it is a shiny gold buckle with a capital *B* for Buckley. Before going on, take a moment or two to see this picture vividly. Forehead, buckle, *Buckley.*

Second, you met Mr. Okimoto. He has bushy eyebrows, and the locomotive is slowly but noisily steaming across his forehead from one eyebrow to the other, disappearing into it. Eyebrows, locomotive, *Okimoto.*

Next you met Miss Siegel. She has big wide nostrils, and her loud sneezes produce hundreds of noisily flapping sea gulls, which fly out of those nostrils. See it now! Nostrils, sea gulls, *Siegel.*

Next you met Miss Wideikis. She has full lips, which you exaggerate into superbig red lips—ready to kiss everything in sight—which she does including you. Full red lips, WID' A KISS, *Wideikis.*

Next, you met Mr. Mahler with the big ears and the dollars. "In one ear and out the other," says laughing, jovial Mahler as he pushes Mahler's DOLLARS in one EAR, and you watch them come out the other. " 'Ear's a dollar for Mahler." Ears, dollar, *Mahler.*

Next, you met Mr. Deiro, pronounced Darrow, like arrow. You noticed the wart on his face. Suddenly, in it is stuck an arrow that found its mark. See it now. Wart, arrow, *Deiro.*

Next you met Ms. Peterson. You notice her stunning smile

and perfect white teeth. You formed your own name and face cues and connections for Ms. Peterson and the following three people. See your connections vividly, now.

Next you met Mr. Nicholas. He has a thick, dark moustache and a widow's peak. You used one of then. See your connections clearly.

Next you met Miss Collins. Miss Collins is old but sprightly. She has many deep wrinkles on her face.

Last, you met Mr. Charise. Mr. Charise has a deep cleft in his chin.

Now that you have reviewed your connections, you are ready for a quiz to see how well you remember these ten people and their names. If you actually met these ten people in person, then saw them a second time, the first thing you would notice would be the same outstanding feature you noticed before.

I will mention this facial feature for each person you met so that you can see it in your mind's eye, as before. This face cue is all you need to bring back to your mind's eye your previous mental picture, the name cue, and finally the name for each person. *The face will tell you the name.* Just let it happen. Write each person's name on the lines to the right.*

Person #1 As soon as you see him, you notice his big ears.
What is the name? _____

Person #2 has thick, bushy eyebrows.
What is the name? _____

Person #3 has full red lips.
What is the name? _____

Person #4 has a high, shiny forehead.
What is the name? _____

Person #5 has flaring nostrils.
What is the name? _____

* Correct answers are listed on page 237. Check yourself now.

Person #6 has a wart on his cheek.
What is the name? _____

Person #7 has a cleft in his chin.
What is the name? _____

Person #8 has a dark moustache and a widow's peak.
What is the name? _____

Person #9 has many deep facial wrinkles.
What is the name? _____

Person #10 has a stunning smile with perfect white teeth.
What is the name? _____

I wouldn't be surprised at all if you remembered all ten names correctly. If you participated fully, it would be surprising if you missed more than one or two.

The more you practice converting, connecting, and reviewing, the easier remembering names will become and the more confidence you will have in your new memory skills. Remember that you only read descriptions of the people you just met in a book. They were not real, three-dimensional people standing in front of you. The CCR System will be far easier for you to apply with living, breathing people.

If you missed more than two or three names in the quiz above, it was because you were not attentive enough, because your pictures were not vivid enough, or because you did not follow the instructions exactly. Like any worthwhile skill, memory skills take time and practical use to develop. It is really the use of the CCR system with real people that provides the best practice. Just *do* it and keep doing it, and you will be delighted with yourself and the results.

The Reason You Remembered These Names As Well As You Did. Normally, before this, if you had met ten new people, you probably wouldn't have remembered more than one or two names, if that many. The reason you have just remembered as many of the ten people in our present exercise as you have, is very simple:

1. You paid attention.
2. You used a memory technique to make it easier for your memory to do the job.

In short, *you really tried* to remember them, you intended to remember them, and you did!

HOW TO PRACTICE WITH THE CCR SYSTEM

A good way to practice remembering names with this system, and to keep your CCR skills sharp, is to practice the Convert-Connect-Review sequence wherever you happen to be. For example, if you happen to be in a restaurant or other place with lots of people around you, just mentally assign each of them a name. Any name will do, as long as it isn't too simple. After you convert, connect, and review them, look at each one again and recall the names.

Another way to practice in spare moments is to think of friends or relatives, or anyone you know, and practice converting their names into various name cues. Of course, if you are reading a newspaper or magazine with photos and names of people, this is a perfect setup with which to practice your CCR.

EXTRA AIDS TO HELP NAMES STICK

A basic undergirding of Memory Control is William James's principle of diverse and multiple associations. Try to use at least one more associative connection each time you form a mental picture to remember something. Any such extra word association or phrase (even if it is not picturable) is useful and effective in deepening the registration of the name, fact, or idea.

These word associations can be phrases with rhymes, rhymes alone, similar sounds, comparisons, contrasts, metaphors, similes, similar things, slogans, nicknames, allusions, alliterated phrases, quotes—anything that is apt, funny, or fits in any way at all. Use whatever occurs to you. Make up word associations on the spot, repeat them a time or two, and you will find the extra reinforcement to be a powerful memory aid.

Here are some word-association phrases of various types for names.*

Mr. Katz has kittens.
Mr. Old looks young.
Ms. Sweet looks sour.
Mr. Wideman is thin.
Miss Stern looks happy.
Ms. Chub is chubby.
Farrel is a barrel.
Cliff looks mountainous.
Bridget is a midget.
Black blew his stack.
Post is really a ghost.
Baldwin is bald.
Eaton likes to eat.
Thurstone looks thirsty.
Rudd is ruddy.
Seymour has two big eyes.
Parton smokes a carton.
Dolly is jolly.
Pitluck is in the pitts.
Moon is a goon.
Kirk was a clerk; now
  he's a jerk.
Devereaux will never owe.
Dillon is a villain.
Fox is a fox.
Wolf is a wolf.
Marx makes high marks.

Bowers bakes bananas.
Jensen's jokes are jests.
Drew threw goo.
Snelling is smelling.
Gold is old.
Nickel tickles.
Berry is merry.
Melon is a felon.
Spring is a ding-a-ling.
Mr. Fall is tall.
Sommers is hot stuff.
East is a beast.
North goes forth.
South has a big mouth.
West is best, but won't
  stand the test.
Block is a rock.
Carson the parson.
Monee has a Sony.
Peevey has a teevie.
Grey is here to stay.
Green is a bean.
Red looks dead.
Blue is new.
Brown, stay down.
Nutt is nutty, not nuts.
Rickles likes pickles.

*Note: These extra associations can easily and profitably be used with the SALT System for remembering names, as well as with the CCR System.

RIGHT BRAIN—LEFT BRAIN

These days, a lot of attention in psychology is being given to the "split-brain" theory. Current findings show that we have woefully neglected the right brain hemisphere, which has to do with imagination, creativity, and intuition. We are too preoccupied with logic, reasoning, and other more rigid disciplines which are now known to originate in the left side of the brain.

Since most mnemonic thinking involves the right side of the brain, the use of memory techniques stimulates creativity and imagination.

FIRST NAMES

We have concentrated on last names so far because they are usually more important than first names. Try to look up a Mary or a Tom in any phone book, and you will soon understand what I mean. First names are handled exactly as we handled last names. They are just as convertible, or even more so because they are shorter than many last names, and there are far fewer of them.

Suppose Mr. Buckley's name is Joe Buckley. Instead of picturing only the buckle, you add a *cup of coffee* ("Joe") to your mental picture. You could see Joe Buckley's shiny gold belt buckle sliding off his forehead into a hot cup of coffee. You might even hear him saying, "Buck up with some coffee," or "Buckle up the coffee cup." If his name were Frank Buckley, you could picture a hot dog (Frank) stuck on that gold buckle. Oscar Buckley could be represented by a gold movie Oscar, which is part of the gold buckle on Buckley's forehead.

If Miss Siegel's (sea gull) first name is Violet, just see violet-colored sea gulls. If her first name is Ginger or Sherry, you could see the flapping sea gulls with ginger cookies in their mouths or poking into glasses of sherry. In the nutshell, if the first name has meaning, use it as is in your mental picturing. If the first name has no meaning, convert it into something meaningful and use this name cue in your picture association.

To give you more examples of first name conversions, here is a sample list of both feminine and masculine first names, with conversions that might be used.

Female First Names

April: a bill, a thrill, Ape-
   ill
Angela: angel
Barbara: barber, a barb
Bea: bee
Belle: bell
Cathy: catty, catheter
Clarice: clear ice
Diana: piana (piano)
Ethel: gasoline (ethyl)
Florence: floor-ants
Gertrude: dirt-rude
Hazel: hazelnut
Ida: cider
Jean: jeans
June: prune
Kate: gate
Lilly: lily
Marge: march
Nell: bell, hell
Olivia: olive
Pat: patina, hat
Ruth: tooth, booth
Sylvia: silver
Terry: towel (terry cloth)
Una: lunar, tuner
Violet: violet (see the color)
Veronica: harmonica
Vivian: Vivitar
Winnie: whinnie (hear the
   sound)

Male First Names

Art: art, dart, cart, chart
Archie: bow and arrow,
   Archie Bunker
Barney: barn
Clark: Clark Gable, clock
David: slingshot
Ellery: celery
Everest: Mount Everest
Frank: frankfurter
George: gorge, forge
Graham: cracker, Billy
   Graham
Harry: hairy, Harry
   Belafonte
Henry: hen with ring, Henry
   Kissinger
Herbert: pervert
Humphrey: Bogart, camel
   (hump)
Jim: gym
Joe: coffee, glow, toe, sew
Keith: keys
Leo: lion
Nick: nickel
Otto: a toe
Peter: heater
Russ: rust
Ray: ray (flashlight beam)
Rick: rickshaw
Sam: Uncle Sam
Stuart: stew

Female First Names

Male First Names

Yolanda: your land
Zelda: zealot

Tom: tomato, tom cat
Van: van
Vic: vicar, Vicks
William: a will
Zeke: peak (Pike's Peak)

Some people have first and last names that are instantly meaningful and picturable in themselves. For example, one of my seminar students was Warren Peese, an architect. As soon as I heard his name, I pictured Tolstoy's book, *War and Peace*. Then I pictured the book on top of a skyscraper, and it became a full-name cue and an occupation cue as well:

WARREN PEESE   ARCHITECT
(War and Peace)   (Skyscraper)
Full-Name Cue   Occupation Cue

I met a man named Otto Horne, and in my mind's eye he became an autohorn. Two other memory students were Lauren Mauer and Violet Organa. I pictured Lauren Mauer with a lawn mower and Violet Organa playing a violet-colored organ. All you have to do to come up with full-name retrieval cues, as with any other type, is to observe the names you hear. Don't just hear them; *observe them*.

You see and hear
With your eye and ear
But you only observe with the mind.

By closely observing names, you can discover various possibilities that might otherwise remain hidden. Remember the ROAM (*R*ecognize *O*r *A*dd *M*eaning) formula? Mentally ROAM around each name you hear (first names, last names, or both names), to see what you can come up with.

Here is what some of my memory students came up with when I asked them what meaning they could observe in, picture in, or associate with the names of the following celebrities:

Name	Full-Name Cue
Jack Lemmon	Cash for lemons
Chevy Chase	Chased by a Chevy
Johnny Cash	Commode with money in it
Dyan Cannon	Dynamite in cannon
Julie London	Jewels of London
Racquel Welch	The racket belched
Marlon Brando	A marlin drinking brandy
Muhammad Ali	More ham in the alley
Goldie Hawn	Moldy lawn
Gore Vidal	A bore withal
Julie Christie	Cool and misty
Shelley Winters	Smelly splinters
Cloris Leachman	Clorox bleach
Don Knotts	The godfather is nuts
Luciano Pavarotti	Lucy on a paved potty
Rock Hudson	Rock in Hudson River
John Voigt	Toilet bowl empty
Robert Redford	Robber in a red Ford
Red Buttons	Red buttons
Redd Foxx	Red fox
Red Skelton	Red skeleton
George Burns	George burns

APPLYING THE CCR SYSTEM
DURING CONVERSATION

If you have wondered how easy it is to apply this system while conversing with someone, you can relax. This is not a problem. After you have heard the name clearly in the beginning, and you repeat it and spell it, you use the technique of asking questions.

Just ask appropriate conversational questions, and let the other person do most of the talking while you form your name and face cues and connect them.

Any personal questions, such as, "What is it like in your home town?" or "What's the weather like in your area?" or "What are some of the things you do in your line of work?" or especially, "Tell me about your children" are the kinds of open-ended questions that will give you the time you need to apply the CCR System. In the beginning, try not to ask questions that can be answered by just yes or no. The whole idea is to keep in control of the conversation while you are converting, connecting, and reviewing in your mind. If you are not in a hurry, you can spend as much time as you like with each person you meet and take your time applying the CCR sequence. With some practice you will develop speed, and you will be amazed at how quickly you can meet and remember a succession of people. Just try to keep the beginning of the conversation under control with appropriate questions. The rest will take care of itself. *All of your doubts will disappear as you develop skill with this system.*

STRATEGIES FOR MEETING AND REMEMBERING GROUPS OF PEOPLE

In the same way that you can control each one-on-one conversation by asking the appropriate questions, you can also comfortably control situations that involve large groups. For example, you might be introduced to a succession of people too quickly. Or, despite your best efforts, you could find that you have forgotten a name or names when confronted with several people at once. Both of these things can happen, but they are easily handled with a little forethought and planning.

Take the first situation—control over the speed of introductions. If your hostess grabs you, hustles you over to a group, and with the speed of light introduces you to a dozen people, you can take control so that you can remember everyone's name. The first rule is to get rid of the "introducer." Just politely say that you know how busy he or she is and that you will meet everyone yourself. In all probability, you will be doing the host or hostess, as well as yourself, a favor. Now you can meet people as quickly or slowly as you wish as you comfortably convert, connect, and review. The secret is to meet people one at a time, at your own pace.

If you know in advance that you are going to encounter a large number of people, it is a very good idea to arrive early and meet them one by one, before chaos sets in. Finally, the most important single factor is *to review your connections*, early and often, until you feel sure that the names have "clicked in your mind."

At first, do your reviews after every one, two, or three people you meet. Remember that the more you use the CCR approach, the faster and easier it will become for you, and the more people you can meet before each review. Remember that review is retention!

One more item: Honesty is the best policy. If you look over the people during your reviews and realize that you have lost a name or two, simply tell the person openly and honestly that you seem to have lost his or her name, and ask for it again. You might even say that you are teaching yourself to remember names and it is important to you to remember his or hers. Most people will be flattered, and you will have their names. This time review and strengthen the connections more securely.

These strategies will help you cope with such situations. My students have devised the word COPE as an acronym to remind them of the basics of meeting people in groups:

Come early.
One at a time is how you meet people.
Pace is to be established by you—no one else.
Early reviews, as often as necessary.

Remember the importance of *review*, the third letter in the CCR approach to remembering names. It is the one thing that is usually stressed the least but it is the most important.

- Review to remember.
- Remember to re*view*.

My motto is, "The way to teach is to practice what you preach." With this in mind, we will now *review* the main points and procedures of the SALT and CCR systems.

REVIEW AND SUMMARY

SALT and CCR are systematic Memory Control procedures for registration, retention, and retrieval of names and faces.

Our working concept in this book is Memory Control. The specific Memory Control techniques discussed in this chapter are SALT and CCR. Each is a systematic sequence for control of registration, retention, and retrieval of names.

The SALT System

The SALT System is short, simple, and basic. It enables you to hear the name clearly and get it right the first time around. SALT is a commonsense procedure, using attention, simple repetition, and multisensory registration.

You *say and spell the name, ask a question using the name, learn the name initially by repeating it appropriately during the conversation,* and *terminate the conversation by using the name once more.*

S = *S*AY and *S*PELL
A = *A*SK
L = *L*EARN
T = *T*ERMINATE

The purpose of the SALT acronym is to hold these steps in mind for you so that you remember to follow them until the sequence becomes automatic.

The CCR System (Convert-Connect-Review)

The CCR System is a complete procedure for remembering names and faces:

- You *convert* the name and face into meaningful retrieval cues.
- You *connect* them mentally so that they become virtually inseparable.
- You *review* these connections for reinforcement.

The result is reliable recall of names.
This is accomplished in five specific steps:

1. Get the name clearly! Follow the letter *S* of the SALT System.
2. Give the name meaning for your memory to grasp and hold (the name cue).
3. Pick a facial feature that is striking or noticeable (the face cue).
4. Mentally associate the name cue with the face cue in a *vivid* way.
5. Reinforce this impression with systematic review.

Name Conversion has as its purpose:

1. the creation of a name cue based on the *sound* of the name
2. the creation of a *visual image* for the name so that every name can be *seen* as well as heard

Names fall into three categories:

1. names with meaning
2. reminder names
3. blanks (no-meaning names)

Name Conversion Techniques:

1. The ROAM formula: *R*ecognize *O*r *A*dd *M*eaning
2. The SRS formula: *S*imilar sound, *R*hyme, or *S*eparate syllables

The USA Formula for vivid mental picturing:

U = the *U*nusual, the outstanding (either bizarre or plausible).
S = *S*ee it and hear it vividly in your mind's eye and ear.
A = *A*ction—active interaction between the name cue and the face cue.

Reviewing for Reinforcement:

- Review consolidates the conversion and connection.
- Review to remember. Remember to *review*.

The COPE Formula for meeting people in groups:

Come early.
One at a time is how you meet people.
Pace is to be established by you—no one else.
Early reviews, as often as necessary.

The CCR System at a Glance

1. Upon meeting a person, you convert, connect, and review retrieval cues.
2. Upon seeing the person again, the face cue retrieves the name cue, and the name cue gives you the name.

Names in the Nutshell

Thought determines what you want
But only action determines what you get.

It is not enough to want to remember names better. Action is required with the SALT and CCR methods. To remember names better you must *learn* them better. You have probably had difficulty with names in the past because you didn't know how to learn them effectively in the first place.

The methods you have learned in this chapter will enable you to effectively register, retain, and recall any name or names you may encounter in the future.

8

Making It Stick: Adhesive Tape for the Mind

But this forming of associations with a fact, what is it but thinking about the fact as much as possible? Briefly, then, of two men with the same outward experiences, and the same amount of mere native tenacity, the one who thinks over his experiences most, and weaves them into systematic relations with each other, will be the one with the best memory.

*William James**

An important question you probably want to ask at this point is, "How long can I remember names with the CCR System?" The answer is that you can remember names as long as you want to—for a day, a week, a month, or years—depending on the following factors:

1. the original vividness of your conversion, connection, and review
2. how much importance that person has for you and how much you want to remember him or her

*William James, *Principles of Psychology*, vol. 1 (New York: Henry Holt & Co., 1890), p. 662.

115

3. how well you are willing to reinforce your impression of the name

There is no other realistic answer to the question. Some things can be remembered for a lifetime after only one exposure, but most of the time the knowledge you pick up along the way is very forgettable. This knowledge will disappear unless you know what to do about it and then do it!

It is only within the last fifteen years or so that some of the age-old mysteries of memory have been probed with some success. The "dual memory" theory, a hypothesis that has fascinated memory researchers for some time, states that the brain has both a temporary and a permanent memory system and that they constantly interact. The temporary system is called *short-term memory* (STM), and the permanent is called *long-term memory*, or LTM.

In 1971 Atkinson and Shiffrin produced some landmark research in a paper called "The Control of Short-Term Memory."* In it they showed that by controlling your short-term memory you can direct the transfer of information into and out of your long-term memory storage, *thereby governing all learning and retrieval of information*. This knowledge was enlightening and important, and it set the stage for the concept of personal Memory Control.

You can think of your short-term memory as a kind of mental scratchpad. On it you mentally jot down quick notes about things for immediate thought or action; a telephone number, for example. But seconds later, this number can be forgotten. It disappears from your mind just before, during, or after you dial that number. If this has happened to you, you know the exasperation you feel at such a moment.

Of course, you might repeat the number a few times to keep it in mind; but even if you do, that number can still be as slippery

*Richard C. Atkinson and Richard M. Shiffrin, "The Control of Short-Term Memory," *Scientific American*, August 1971, pp. 82-90.

as an eel and can neatly disappear again, especially if a sudden distraction interrupts your concentration. Such interference can totally wipe out the number from your mind.

YOUR WORKING MEMORY

Short-term memory can best be defined as your conscious mind. Whatever you are consciously aware of at any given moment is in your short-term memory. Since you cannot work with a fact, idea, or other information unless you are first conscious of it, you can also think of your conscious or short-term memory as your working memory.

Each hour or day brings with it an endless succession of thoughts, ideas, and facts that you are conscious of from moment to moment. If you do not select specific thoughts or facts to think about or repeat to yourself, they are easily forgotten. Usually, any item in your short-term memory may stay in consciousness for seconds before some other thought takes its place. Current research shows that short-term memory may last as long as about thirty seconds, but that long-term memory may begin at thirty seconds and last up to a lifetime.

In the same way that you think of your short-term or working memory as your conscious mind, think of your *long-term memory* as your *subconscious mind.*

Consciously thinking of a particular fact or idea gives you the time to code the material so that it can be transferred to your long-term, subconscious memory storage. It is interesting to realize that only one of two things can happen to any fact or idea in your conscious, working, short-term memory. This fact or idea is either forgotten, usually in a matter of seconds, or transferred into your long-term memory—one or the other. The choice is yours; your conscious mind is under your direct control! *You* are the only one who decides to continue thinking about an idea, to associate it with something else or to let some other thought replace it. If you deliberately keep a thought in mind by thinking about it, repeating it, or forming a meaningful mental image of it, *you can create as many long-term memories as you choose*. The point to remember is that through such deliberate direction of your conscious mind, *you* gain control over what is to be remembered or forgotten.

Whatever information you thus transfer to your long-term memory stays there. Your subconscious, long-term memory is your permanent memory file. If you file a fact or idea there in an organized or systematic manner, with meaningful associative connections or retrieval cues, it will be far easier to recall when you need it. If you do not file it with deliberate associative connections of some sort, it will be more difficult to recall. Whether or not you make deliberate associations, your mind will still form its own connections, but these associations or retrieval-cues will be harder for you to find later on because your conscious mind did not originally create them. This is why deliberately memorizing and recalling names, facts, and numbers, with specific associative memory techniques, is so much easier than trying to remember them without a system.

As you know from your previous experience with the CCR System for names, retrieval cues quickly locate such memorized material in your long-term memory and transfer it back to your conscious mind. It is then ready for use until you are finished with it. This material is then instantly retransferred to your subconscious, long-term memory, where it awaits activation by a future retrieval cue.

This constant interchange between your short-term and long-term memory constitutes the continuous, moment-to-moment, day-by-day functioning of your memory.

At Yale University Endel Tulving's work showed that forgetting is not a problem of retention but of retrieval. We do not necessarily forget at all. Rather, we experience *retrieval failure* because we have difficulty in finding the right retrieval cues to locate and release hidden information, which, though still in long-term memory, remains inaccessible. It is available, but not accessible. Trying to recall a name, or number, or an idea from your long-term memory is like trying to locate a book in a large library. The fact that you cannot find the book doesn't mean it isn't there. You may simply be looking on the wrong shelf or in the wrong section, or the book might simply be misplaced, making it inaccessible. Many forgotten memories are not really lost, but they are difficult to reach if you do not have the correct retrieval cue.

Perfect Memory/Imperfect Access

Many people talk about their "poor memories" as though their inability to remember a name or a fact were due to their inability to "retain." "My memory is like a sieve," they complain, as though it cannot "hold" anything. Actually, most memory psychologists believe that as long as there is no injury to the brain, every individual's retention is probably perfect.

Research continually shows that a failure of memory almost always boils down to a failure in the retrieval stage. A common example is when you can't think of the correct answer in an exam you are taking, but later, when you least need it, the answer pops into mind. The tip-of-the-tongue phenomenon is another example: You know that a name or number or other fact is tantalizingly "there," but you just can't recall it. This is all clear evidence that the material is still in your memory, but that for some reason it remains inaccessible.

The techniques of Memory Control work with retrieval cues that permit direct access to material so committed to memory. Unlike memorization by rote repetition, which demands time and effort, Memory Control's direct access permits rapid retention and recall through meaningful associative connections. If you remember those connections, you remember the material. It is as simple as that. However, not everything can be memorized through such a systematic approach, nor is a system always needed. With this in mind, it is very important to remember that the best way to keep any learned information accessible is to *use it* now and then so that it can remain both available and accessible.

REMEMBERING MR. WHATSHISNAME

When you meet a succession of people in the same way, saying, "Nice to meet you," to each one, you can easily forget each name in *seconds*. On the other hand, taking the time to code and transfer each name properly from your short-term to your long-term memory makes all the difference.

By converting, connecting, and reviewing your associations, you are consolidating the name and face impressions, and you are enabling them to be coded into your long-term memory storehouse. *This momentary effort of coding is what transfers names or other items into long-term memory.*

You would do well to remember this, because it is exactly and specifically the way you deliberately initiate and complete that transfer. Here is a review of the basic steps for getting materials from your short-term to your long-term memory:

1. Choose the items that are important to you and that you want and intend to remember.
2. Code the material into a more meaningful form so that your memory can grasp and hold it long enough to make the transfer. All the techniques in this book are designed to accomplish this.
3. Realize that the mental effort *itself* in step 2 is what transfers the material into your long-term memory.

If you grasp the full significance of step 3, you will know something of inestimable value, which relatively few people realize, and you will be way ahead in the pages to follow.

It goes without saying that it is not necessary to deliberately code all information in order to remember it. Many things that are very meaningful or important to you are remembered after only one exposure, without use of systematic memory techniques. Some of these are things you may *never* forget; they are things that just seem to "remember themselves": Your own name, the names of your loved ones, your birthday, and your first date are examples. As for these names, you use them so often that repetition and use alone make them unforgettable. As for your first date, or your high school graduation, or the first time you experienced *anything* important, such things are usually remembered.

It is also quite possible to hear a name or fact just once and never forget it. In psychology this is called *one-trial learning.* For example, if you are meeting a man whose name is Hofner, and he suddenly strikes you across the face, *instantly* his name, his face, and everything about him is automatically transferred from your short-term to your long-term memory. You don't have to take notes, review, or use a memory system. Such a transfer takes place all by itself because the event is so outstanding. Because of this, you will probably never forget that man or the name Hofner.

That example involved a physical event; but words, facts, and ideas can be transferred just as quickly to your long-term memory. Suppose you suddenly receive the news that a rich uncle just died and left you $10 million! Would you—could you—ever forget it, or that moment?

Here is the point: Very few facts, names, numbers, ideas, and experiences are, in themselves, so outstanding to you that they are instantly and automatically transferred to long-term memory. Since they are not so transferred, such impressions stay in your conscious mind for a matter of seconds and are then forgotten. This is exactly why you forget so many things in day-to-day living. And, as for those important things that you "should have remembered," you didn't *do* anything about them, so they were forgotten too.

WHO NEEDS A SYSTEM?

Of course at this point you can say that you know people who seem to remember names with no trouble at all, without getting "hit in the face" and without using any memory system. Undoubtedly, you could cite another friend who is a whiz at remembering numbers and statistics, and another who can easily quote any page in the Bible—again, without the aid of memory aids or systems.

This is quite likely. However, if you ever went to the trouble of figuring out what enables such people to remember things so well, I think you would find that such people do indeed use a system. The system they use may seem different from the applied control techniques you are learning here, yet it is very similar in essence. Such people may not deliberately convert, connect, and review with a formal procedure, but what they actually do amounts to the same thing and produces the same results. First, they pay attention! (If they didn't, they would remember nothing.) These people usually find other people naturally interesting, including their names and everything else about them. They listen to and learn about the person they are meeting, and whether they know it or not, as they converse their minds are busy forming interesting associations, comparisons, and contrasts with other people they know who have similar interests and occupations. All of these connections occur *because* of their attentiveness and interest.

They may find that they have mutual friends or that they have a hobby or other interests in common; they may discuss a play or concert or movie they have both attended. All of these associations and connections register as a natural result of attention and interest, which in turn encourages a more meaningful conversation and exchange of ideas. In this way the new acquaintance cannot help but become more meaningful and memorable. All of this must inevitably result in naturally better registration and recall of the person and his or her name, as well as many other interesting facts about the individual.

Attention is the first requirement. But also becoming interested (even for the moment) in the person you are meeting can perform miracles. And it does so without methodical procedures, as with a system.

When genuine interest is present a good mental impression of a name follows almost automatically. The catch is that it isn't always easy for you to be genuinely interested in the things you would like to remember. In these cases, the deliberate application of a systematic memory procedure saves the day. It does so by accomplishing the same thing that natural interest does, but via a different route.

What the CCR System (or any other system in this book) does is to force you to pay attention and mentally manipulate the name, fact, or idea in such a way that it is grasped and held by your mind and memory. Through such coding it is successfully and *deliberately* transferred to your long-term memory.

Again, people who remember names without memory aids or systems often do other things that produce equally reliable results in remembering names. It is not uncommon for such people to write names down and keep systematic records of all those they wish to remember. Before the next anticipated meeting they review these written records and even study photos of various people met in the past. I have seen people go through the motions of writing down the name, using a forefinger to trace the letter on their palm in order to visualize the name and reinforce it.

So, people who seem to just "naturally" remember names, are largely a figment of our imagination. We believe what we wish to believe about them, but many of them are the first to admit that they have to *work* at remembering names. In the last analysis, what they really do is to take the time and effort to make sure that they learn the names they want to remember. Such people rarely complain of a faulty memory for names.

In short, a good memory for names is really a matter of what you *do*, rather than of what you *have*. So, if you haven't been remembering names as well as other people you know, it is quite probable that you simply do not go to the same trouble that they do. There are no poor memories; there are only poor learning habits.

HOW TO REMEMBER NAMES FOR GOOD

The answer is effective reinforcement! I'm going to give you plain and practical, commonsense reinforcement ideas for making sure that you do remember the names of those you want to remember.

The first thing to do is to write the name down some time after the original meeting, certainly before you feel that you may forget it. This is for people you want to remember, want to see, or expect to see as time goes by. I suggest using 3-by-5-inch cards in a small file box for this purpose. On each card it is best to write down not only the name, address, phone number, and other vital information, but also the name cue and face cue you used and how you connected them. It's also a good idea to jot down any other items you think of that will help you clearly picture him or her in your mind's eye.

Keep these written reminders where you can reach them for a quick review whenever necessary, especially right before you expect to see that person again. Many successful people keep just such an alphabetized card file of names and facts about people met, for future review and reinforcement. Again, it's only common sense.

MEMORY MAINTENANCE—THE *TRU* FORMULA

The TRU Formula provides the best answer to reinforcing not only names, but anything and everything else you would like to remember. The TRU Formula is applied common sense, which, in the memory department, always works best. This TRU Formula will work to reinforce connections and mental pictures you have made previously, or, in many cases, it can be used by itself, without any memory control technique.

TRU is an acronym for *T*hink, *R*epeat, and *U*se:

T = *T*hink about the name, fact, or data you want to remember. Merely thinking about the information now and then is repetition and reinforcement in itself. Think of other associations for the material. The more connections, the better. Remember William James's principle of diverse associations.

Compare and contrast the information with other similar or contrasting data. A *very* effective reinforcement is to come up with questions starting with *what, when, where, who, why,* and *how,* in relation to the items you want to reinforce.

R = *R*epeat, review, recite. All of these should be done as soon and as often as your need, interest, and inclination permit. In studying, reciting is an especially powerful reinforcement tool. Remember that whenever you recite something you are actually rehearsing future retrieval. Another high-potential reinforcement tool for study is the ARC Method, described later.

U = *U*se. Use the name, fact, number, or idea. Try not to let it just "sit there." Keep it active whenever you can by actually telling that joke or using that phone number, quotation, new word, anecdote, or new fact you want to keep in mind. Use whatever you want to remember in conversation or at any other kind of opportunity. This simple use of the item now and then will make it a lifelong usable possession. All information is potentially forgettable. In general, what you don't use you lose.

In short, how easily or how long you remember something depends on how often you retrieve it. The more often you use it, the more accessible it becomes.

> The rules of remembering are three
> And all others are in vain.
> The first and second are *use it*—
> And the third is *use it again.*

When it comes to remembering, it is up to U. (*U*se it!) So there you have the TRU formula for long-lasting memory reinforcement. It all boils down to this:

PRACTICE MAKES PERMANENT—
That's the trick
Of making it stick.

9

A Working Memory for Things to Do: The Art of Mental Filing

No matter what your job or daily routine involves, there is one special type of remembering that is important and necessary to everyone. All of us have certain things that should or must be done during the day, and we have only three possible courses of action: to do those things, to delay, or to discard them altogether. So often, many of the things that are discarded are really just forgotten; many times, forgetting to do such things can produce dire consequences. Forgetting to mail a letter might not create much of a problem (unless it is your income tax return), but forgetting to make a plane reservation or to get a birthday present for a family member can have serious repercussions. Since it is often human nature to remember the negative things more than the positive, it seems likely that your boss, or associates, or friends, or even your family members may remember you most often for the things you forget to do rather than for the things you remember. There is an old saying:

When I do something right, no one remembers.
When I do something wrong, no one forgets.

The person who forgets a telephone number may be thought of as having an unreliable memory; but the person who forgets to make the phone call may be thought of as an unreliable person. When it comes right down to it, most people forget to do things because they do not have a practical and easy system that effectively *reminds* them to do what has to be done. The result is that many things, including priority items, are forgotten.

To remember all those "things to do," most people resort to writing themselves notes. This is usually a good idea, and I recommend making notes whenever possible. If you have a desk pad, use it. If you have a sales book, pocket secretary, or pocket note pad, you should certainly use them. Unfortunately, there are certain times when you simply cannot write things down. As a result, important ideas, facts, appointments, or other priorities are simply lost in the shuffle.

For many people, it is important to capture good ideas as they occur. If you do not have an alternate method of catching these ideas before they are gone, they are usually gone for good. A good idea may come to you in the middle of the night for that important staff meeting tomorrow morning, or you may suddenly have a great idea while you are driving on the freeway. In cases like these, of course, you could still take the trouble to make a notation, but most people don't. It is usually easier to decide just to try to "remember it" later.

Such haphazard, hit-or-miss memory habits are very expensive in the long run. Still, most people just never stop to think of the importance of systematic reminders or the things usually forgotten without them. The systems you are about to learn can make you far more efficient and productive; they will help you manage your time better in general.

What I am going to teach you now is how to remember the things you want and need to remember but usually have difficulty in remembering, especially when you cannot write these things down. It is exactly in these situations that Mental Filing Systems shine.

YOUR MENTAL NOTEBOOK

Used properly, Mental Filing Systems allow you to write things in your mind instead of on paper. All you do is file them, review them, and retrieve them as necessary. The systems themselves are easy and fast acting; they work anytime, anyplace; they are erasable; and they can be used over and over again indefinitely. These systems are mental holding devices; they hold information in formation. They trap information of all kinds and store it in your memory in such a way that you can systematically locate the specific items and get them back out again at will.

A mental filing system is exactly what the term implies. It works just like the filing system in an office except that you always have it with you, and it frees you from slavery to your written notes. You can instantly mentally file a fact or idea for future discussion or a reminder to do a specific thing during the day. If the mentally filed information is something you want to get down on paper, your mental file will hold it for you until you have a chance to write it down.

HOW DO MENTAL FILING SYSTEMS WORK?

The systems are simple in concept and work quickly and smoothly with a bit of practice. They are based on the universal reminder principle, the retrieval cue. You will remember that the retrieval cue is the basic unit in all Memory Control techniques and systems.

Just as with remembering names, faces, where you put things, and telephone numbers, you set up and operate retrieval cues that store, retain, and later deliver all information so processed. The mental file systems you are about to learn are all organized, preset sequences of specially constructed retrieval cues. As soon as you learn the sequence, you can start to file things in your mind.

THE PAR TECHNIQUES

In remembering names and faces, we used the CCR System (Convert, Connect, and Review). Although the conversion idea is used in mental filing, more often it is unnecessary because so many of the items you file are mentally picturable in their original form. In mental filing we use the PAR Formula, which describes the three techniques involved:

P = *P*icture it.
A = *A*ssociate it.
R = *R*eview it.

As a general reminder, PAR also means *P*ay *A*ttention and *R*emember!

In office files, the two systems used most often for labeling file folders are the alphabetical and numerical methods. A letter from the Ambrose Corporation is simply filed under *A*. Later, when the letter is needed, the file clerk simply thinks of *A* for Ambrose, looks in the file under *A*, finds the letter, and successfully retrieves it.

- The typing on the paper itself is the *registration*.
- Storing the letter in the file under letter "A" is the *retention*.
- Taking the letter back out of the file is the *retrieval*.

Just as you control these three Rs of registration, retention, and retrieval in office filing, you control your mental processing (mental filing) of these three Rs in the same way. Think of it as systematic mental storage and retrieval of information.

THE BODY FILE

To get you started quickly and easily in mental filing, we will first use your body itself as a portable file. Instead of filing things under letters or numbers (as you will in subsequent mental filing systems), you will first learn literally to file things on top of your head, in your pocket, in your hands, and even in your nose.

Our first six bodily file places are easily remembered in order by simply thinking of them as being "from the top of your head to the tips of your toes" (or more simply, "from top to bottom").

- Hair
- Nose
- Mouth
- Hands
- Pocket
- Foot

It is important to remember the exact sequence of these six places; so look at them and study them for a moment and then repeat them a few times to yourself, *touching* each place as you name it for sensory reinforcement. Continue to do this a few times and then mentally go over those six file places, visualizing each in your mind's eye without any touching. Please do not continue until you have learned these first six file places.

The next six file places are in the *spaces* around your body:

- To your *left*
- To your *front*
- To your *right*
- To your *back*
- *Above* you
- *Below* you

It is easy to remember the directional flow of these locations if you think of them as an "uncompleted circle" starting from your left and continuing to your front, right, and back. As for above and below, they are easy enough just to remember in themselves. Now, for the next minute or so, memorize the order of these last six body spaces.

Below is the complete body file. Repeat it to yourself without looking at the page until you know it cold and can instantly visualize all twelve file places in the correct sequence:

- Hair
- Nose
- Mouth
- Hands
- Pocket
- Foot
- Left
- Front
- Right
- Back
- Above
- Below

As for *above*, you might visualize the blue sky, the ceiling, or anything else that represents *above* to you. For *below* you could simply picture the floor, the earth, a hole in the ground, or whatever else means *below* to you. Some of my students picture hell or the devil for *below* because it makes a vivid mental picture!

At this point I want to remind you of the USA Formula for vivid mental picturing. The more vividly you see your file placements in your mind's eye, the better and more quickly you will be able to recall each filed item. This is important, so remember to let this USA Formula guide and remind you to make your visualizations as clear as possible.

U = the *U*nusual, exaggerated, striking, unforgettable.

S = *S*ee the picture as vividly as you can for a few seconds. "Hear it, touch it, taste it" when possible.

A = *A*ction! Interact the item you file with its file place. See it happening with action.

To make it easier for you to follow the USA Formula, here are a few action ideas you can use for each of the body-file places:

Hair: Hair blows around; item "stuck" in hair; hair coming out; hair turns colors.

Nose: Sneezes the item out! Sniff item, smell it; item goes in or out of nose; item is hanging from your nose; it covers your nose.

Mouth: Bite the item! Chew it, taste it, swallow it; it protrudes from your mouth; kiss it.

Hands: Squeeze, pat, or juggle the item. Hit it, throw it, or catch it.

Pocket: Item protrudes from your pocket; it jumps in or out of pocket; it "feels" funny; it shakes around inside; it tears the cloth; it feels hot or cold; it makes noise.

Foot: Kick the item! Step on it to hold it; tie it around your ankle; put your foot in it; tap it; push it away; crush it.

Left: See the item growing to your left! See it burning, freezing, falling over. Turn to the left and hug it, touch it, push it. See it move, dance, jump, talk to you, float in the air to the left.

Front: The item is confronting you: it's funny, threatening, melting, turning colors, falling apart, reaching for you, shaking hands with you.

Right: Any of the above for *left* or *front*.

Back: Hear it behind you! It's gaining on you: strange noise, feelings; it's on your back! It is scratching your back; it kicks you.

Above: See it falling toward you from the sky or ceiling; it's flying to you.

Below: See it on the floor; it's rolling, jumping, sliding, coming apart, digging a hole, falling in, exploding.

As you can see, there are many ways to create lively action and vivid clarity for your mental pictures. So use the USA Formula to guide you. It makes all the difference between remembering and forgetting.

MENTAL FILING IN ACTION

Suppose that you have just risen in the morning, and while you are in the shower or while you are shaving you decide to mentally file a few things you want to remember to do during the day. Let's take this step by step so that you can participate now. Follow these simple instructions exactly:

File Place (Retrieval Cue)	Things to Do Today	Mental Filing Procedure
Hair	Reserve Airline Tickets.	Get your first file place in mind, *hair*. Imagine a toy airplane stuck in your hair, buzzing around, trying to fly out. The *propeller* is clipping your hair! See it and feel it for a few seconds. (Later, when you think of the file-cue, *hair*, it will recall the picture you just made, and the airplane will represent "get airline tickets" to you.) So remember: HAIR – AIRLINE TICKETS.
Nose	Mail Your Income Tax.	Now get your second file place, *nose*, in mind. Picture and feel your nose sneezing violently and spraying tacks (tax)— *thumbtacks*—all over everything. You sneeze again and spray *hundreds* of tacks into a white mailing

File Place (Retrieval Cue)	Things to Do Today	Mental Filing Procedure
		envelope, to mail your tacks. Those tacks are sharp. Feel them as you sneeze and spray a hundred more into the white tacks (tax) envelope. Take two or three seconds to see, hear, and feel the action. NOSE – MAIL INCOME TAX.

After finishing your morning routine you drive to work. Some important things occur to you as you drive, so you decide to file them temporarily until you get to work, where you can write them down. You quickly review your mental file places, starting with *hair*, which is being attacked by the buzzing little airplane. Next, you see your *nose* still sneezing out tacks. But at the next file place, your *mouth*, nothing is happening.

File Place (Retrieval Cue)	Things to Do Today	Mental Filing Procedure
Mouth	See Mr. Frank.	Convert the name *Frank* into *frankfurter* and see a fat, foot-long, juicy red frankfurter as you bite it, taste it, and chew it voraciously. It tastes so good that you will be sure to remember to see Mr. Frank later on today, when you look into your mouth file.

File Place	Things to Do Today	Mental Filing Procedure
Hands	Go to the Bank.	Picture a bright red piggybank in your hands. It feels cold from the "cold" cash inside. Feel the cold, red hardness of the metal piggybank in your fingers. See yourself tossing it back and forth from hand to hand and hear the coins jingling. HANDS – PIGGY-BANK. (Go to the bank!)

Mental filing is a Direct Access Retrieval Technique (DART). Each file place is a retrieval cue that permits direct access to all information filed in your memory. However, the more extra cues you use along with the regular file cue, the more hooks you will have to fish up the stored items. So use your imagination to come up with wordplays, such as "cold" cash, "income tacks" (tax), and so on. Such things you think of will give you a chuckle and will buckle down the items in your mind more firmly. In this sense the acronym DART can also mean *Diverse Associations Registration Technique*, based on William James's diverse and multiple associations principle.

File Place (Retrieval Cue)	Things to Do Today	Mental Filing Procedure
Pocket	Make Phone Calls.	Telephone and Pocket: See a shiny yellow telephone sticking out of your pocket! You are using a Pocket-Phone. Now hear it ring-

File Place (Retrieval Cue)	Things to Do Today	Mental Filing Procedure
		ing *inside* your pocket. A shiny yellow pocket-phone ringing and peeking out of your pocket! See it and hear it now. Make those important phone calls!
Foot	Have Car Washed.	Car Wash and Foot: Right now, in your mind's eye, get behind your car, and kick it into the car wash. Keep kicking it with your foot until it is all the way in. When it's shiny and clean, you get your kicks, and you'll have nothing to kick about. Then you can foot the bill. Kick that car into the car wash!

While you are having lunch, or just before you leave the table, mentally review your files so far to see what has been done and what remains to be done before the day is over. Remember the PAR Formula? So far you have done the P and A (*P*icturing and *A*ssociating) segment, but the all-important review should be done now and then during the day to reinforce your retention for retrieval. Periodic review will also serve as a reminder to add new things to do to your files, if necessary.

The three rules of reinforcement are review, review, and review. With this in mind, let's review the six things to do that you have mentally filed so far. Put the book down and think of each of your first six file places, one at a time. Let each one bring back the mental picture connections you made and see if you know what each file place is "telling you" to do. Do this now, before going on.

If you have followed the directions carefully, you should have recalled each of the first six things to do with no difficulty at all. If you did have a bit of trouble, you did not make your picture connections vivid enough. If this happened, go back and mentally refile the six things to do; then retrieve them *successfully* before going on.

After lunch, on the way back to your office, an idea for reducing expenses and increasing productivity suddenly strikes you. You have a pen but no memo pad with you, so you decide to mentally file this important money-saving idea before you lose it. You can always write it down when you get back to work.

File Place (Retrieval Cue)	Things to Do Today	Mental Filing Procedure
Your Left	Turn Extra Storeroom into Another Office.	See yourself at work, standing so that the extra storeroom is to your *left* as you watch and direct the removal of old equipment and the installation of new office furniture. See and hear it all happening to your left. You turn to your left and go in to make sure no old furniture is left. You direct the installation of a left-handed typewriter, a left-handed desk and chairs. There is nothing left to do because nothing was *left* in the *storeroom*.

File Place	Things to Do Today	Mental Filing Procedure
Your Front	Buy Eggs.	Use the file place *front* to file the *eggs* you need to pick up on the way home. Right now, see gooey, slurpy, sticky, yellow egg yolk dripping down your shirt or blouse *front*. It's wet and smelly. You feel *eggy* all over. Better get the *egg* off your *front*! See it now.
Your Right	Buy Kleenex.	Look to your right. It's "snowing" Kleenex! See it as you reach out with your right hand to grab some of that snow-white Kleenex. See yourself grabbing gobs of it by the handful with your *right* hand. KLEENEX to your RIGHT.
Your Back	Buy Butter.	You feel something funny on your *back*, and you realize that someone is giving you a back massage with *butter*. It's warm, and you smell butter. Someone is buttering you up. You turn around to see who it is, and it's Racquel Welch! (Or Robert Redford, as

File Place (Retrieval Cue)	Things to Do Today	Mental Filing Procedure
		the case may be). Some massage. Butter believe it! BACK – BUTTER.
Above	Interview Secretarial Applicants this afternoon.	Surprise! You're on your own for this and the next one.
Below	Make a Dental Appointment.	Use some picture action involving your *dentist*.

You have just mentally filed twelve things to do during the day. Now do the following things in order:

1. Quickly mentally review your complete sequence of twelve *file places only* (not the pictures you made).
2. Now *review* your mental files, calling to mind each of the pictured associations you made. Be sure you know what each one tells you to do.
3. I will now give you a little quiz, with the file cues in scrambled order. As soon as you see each successive file place cue, let it bring back the picture that will remind you to do a specific thing. That specific thing is the correct answer to each of the following. Here are the questions. You provide the answers.
    1. What was filed in your *hands*?
    2. With your *foot*?
    3. To your *front*?
    4. In your *nose*?
    5. *Above* you?
    6. To your *left*?
    7. What is filed with your *mouth*?

8. With your *hair?*
9. With your *pocket?*
10. To your *right?*
11. *Below* you?
12. In *back* of you?

Now that you have the idea, you can make your own personalized body file, if you so choose. You can make it as long or as short as you like. To extend it, just add any other body places you want to use. Use them in any sequence that is easy for you to remember. A body file of twelve places is sufficient for most purposes. I suggest that you do not use too many more file places with this particular system. Succeeding file systems you will learn—the house file, the ABC file—and the original Brain Chain system can be longer, if desired.

You have now used the PAR procedure to store and retrieve practical daily priority items for action. This completes your first experience with Mental Filing.

FILING ABSTRACT IDEAS AND CONCEPTS

When the information you want to hold in your mental files is abstract rather than concrete, it may be difficult for you to picture such material in its original form or wording. This is the time to use the conversion technique, as you did with names and faces and all types of numbers. Such conversions will give specific meaning your memory can grab and picture. For example, you could picture the concept *honesty* by seeing Abraham Lincoln, George Washington, or whomever or whatever represents honesty to you. Your own pictures, associations, and conversions will always work best for you, because you are the one who thinks of them, and therefore you will think of the same things later on at recall.

The concept of *wealth* could be pictured as a roll of hundred-dollar bills, or an overflowing treasure chest, or a wealthy person you know. *Work* can be pictured as someone shoveling snow or a carpenter installing a door. For *education*, you might picture a graduate in cap and gown or a teacher in front of a class or chalkboard.

The following abstract concepts are shown with suggested picturable conversions. They are all workable, and they will retrieve the original concept. These are only the conversions that I think of at this moment. Remember that the ones that occur to you are the best ones for you to use in actual mental filing.

Abstract Idea or Concept	Conversion to Picture Symbol
Love	Valentine or heart
Magic	Magician performing on TV
Talkative	Muhammad Ali
Clean	Mr. Clean (detergent), bathtub, or a shower stall or soap
Crime	Man with a gun
Housing	House
Prison Reform	Prisoner in uniform
Social Security	Social Security card
Poverty	Undernourished, sickly child
Persuasion	Lawyer in front of jury
Depressing	Sickbed with patient
Anxious	Don Knotts, shaking and quivering
Happy	A loved one, smiling and laughing
Inflation	Balloon with dollar sign, getting bigger and bigger
Goodness	Halo
Opportunity	Hand knocking on a door

Abstract Idea or Concept	Conversion to Picture Symbol
Stubborn	Mule
Permanence	Rock of Gibraltar
Idea	Light bulb turning on
Secret	Two people whispering
Awakening	Alarm clock
Efficiency	Fish, efficient swimmer, or "A fish in sea" (Separate Syllables)

With a little imagination, virtually any idea or concept can be visualized as a concrete picture symbol. As you can see, this remarkably useful and effective conversion principle works quite well for other ideas and concepts as well as for names and numbers.

THE HOUSE FILE

Now that you have experienced the effectiveness of the body file, you are prepared to learn the house file, which I consider the best and fastest mental filing system for practical use. The ancient Greeks used a memory system known as the method of *loci* (locations). They would literally take a walk in a familiar area in which they knew the location of a pillar, a stone, a tree, a sign, a building, or any other specific physical object. As they approached each they would mentally picture the fact or idea they wanted to remember interacting with the object. In this way they would place each item to be remembered in its particular location. Later, in order to retrieve this information, they would merely take a mental walk along the same path they took earlier. Each successive landmark (or file place) would then call to mind the information needed.

Famous Greek and Roman orators used this system in order to remember their speeches. They would call each successive point to mind by noting the successive loci in their mental walk. This system proved very effective and was highly regarded and taught as part of rhetoric. This is how the phrases "in the first place" and "in the second place" came into being. This system has stood the test of time. Many professional speakers used it today exactly as I am going to teach it to you. You would do well to learn it.

Basically, instead of using locations on your body, you will be using specific items and locations in your house or apartment. As easy and effective as the body file is, the house file is even more so. Also, there are advantages in having more than one mental filing system at your command. As a matter of fact, I will be teaching you at least four different ones in this chapter. Each of these systems has characteristics that make it suitable for one application or another; the choice of the system and its application is up to you.

Setting Up Your House File

In the same way that you originally learned the body file by memorizing the logical order of body and body space locations, do the same with the house file. The only difference is that you can now use file places (loci, or locations) of *any known sequence of objects* whose order or arrangement is already familiar to you. For example, you could use the sequential order of certain landmarks on your way to work every day, or the order you see in the sequence of positions on the baseball field, or the typical sequence of an American dinner (appetizer, soup, salad, main course, dessert, coffee), or any natural numerical sequence, or even the order of the twenty-six letters of the alphabet. The last two examples, numbers and alphabetical letters, are the basis of two such systems that will be taught later in this chapter.

Because you are already thoroughly familiar with the orderly arrangement of rooms and their various items in your house or apartment, this house file is probably the easiest and fastest of all mental filing systems for most people to use. It is easy for you to picture either the interior or exterior of your home; you know the floor plan, what each room looks like, and the location and orderly sequence of pieces of furniture, appliances, and other household items.

As I enter my house the first things I see are the foyer, some plants, and the guest closet; then come the kitchen, dining room, living room, and the family room down the stairs. In my house file I use various items in these areas in the order in which they appear as I walk through. It is easy and natural for me to visualize all these things in their correct order, and so it will be for you. You can do the same thing once you decide on the areas and items you want to use for your house file.

We used twelve loci (file places) in the body file, though we could have used more or fewer. You could use just the first six file places if you like, as a short file system for a small shopping list, and the last six body spaces as a separate system to be used only for filing study material or specific things to do. These systems are all flexible, and they allow plenty of room for personal ingenuity.

The house file we will set up now will have sixteen locations so that you can remember sixteen separate facts, ideas, or things to do. Once you learn it, you can shorten or lengthen it to fit your own requirements. With the house file you can easily extend the system to fifty or even a hundred or more cue words or file places, and it will still work like a charm. Most other books on memory teach a file system of up to one hundred cues based on a number-letter system. Through the years, this system has acquired various names: the phonetic alphabet, figure alphabet, memory alphabet, letter-number system, number-consonant code, number code, and others. With this system you can know the numerical position of any item you mentally file. But years of experience have shown that very few people ever have the need to know the numerical position of fifty or a hundred mentally filed items. As a matter of fact, a Mental Filing System for most practical purposes does not require more than ten to fifteen file places, and numerical positions are usually irrelevant.

In fact, having to recall a number, its file-cue, and the item filed is a three-step process that takes extra time and mental effort. In the house file, as in the body file, you simply mentally scan your files to see what is there. It is fast and efficient. If you do need to know the numerical position of mentally filed material, you can use the number rhyme file system, which you will also learn in this chapter.

The house file is easier to expand than the body file. If you add too many more file places to your twelve-cue body file, their general similarity, all being body-related, may impair distinct imagery. But in the house file, since all items are more distinctive, confusion stemming from sameness of file places is unlikely.

In my own house file my file place cues begin as I enter the house. However, you may prefer to start your imaging sequence from your bedroom, since it is the first place each day from which you start your daily activities. It doesn't matter. Just decide where you want to have the mental picture sequence start and carry on from there.

I suggest that you select four areas in your home, one leading naturally to the other, with about four items in each area or room serving as your file places or cue word locations. For example, starting in your bedroom, you might select the bed, alarm clock, chair, and dresser as the four file places. These should, of course, be pictured in sequence as you look around your bedroom. In this way, when you take a mental walk through your bedroom, these items will appear in that exact order. It is important for you to think a bit in order to decide on the specific sequence of file places that you want to use for your complete house file.

It is not really necessary to think in terms of a particular sequence of rooms. If it is easier to select sixteen items that appear one by one as you walk in a familiar pattern through your house, do so. The sequence of cue words (file places) themselves is what is important for you to know perfectly.

Now take the time to make up your own house file, in the sequence you choose, on the following sixteen lines.

_____   _____

_____   _____

_____   _____

_____   _____

_____   _____

_____   _____

_____   _____

_____   _____

Once you have decided on the exact sequence of house file places, just go over them mentally, picturing each item in order until you can do so automatically, without hesitation. Then you are ready to use it as a mental filing system. You file, retrieve, and review things exactly as you did in the body file. Once you do this a time or two with the house file, you will find this system even easier to use than the body file.

Extending the House File

If you want to use more than sixteen file places with the house file, it is easy to add additional cue words. You may never need more than the original sixteen, but if you do, just select more items in your house that can easily follow your sixteenth cue word in some logically sequential order. Your house file can contain as many file places as you like. Memory performers who entertain with feats of memory may use fifty to one hundred or more cue words, depending on the type of demonstration. I do not recommend such mental gymnastics. Just concentrate on being practical and effective, not phenomenal.

You may be wondering how long you will be able to remember the information you file mentally. Once you form a mental picture association between the thing you want to remember and your file cue word, it will remain accessible to recall for hours, days, or longer, depending on the vividness of its registration and reinforcement. As we said before, it is a good idea to review your files occasionally during the same day you file the material. This is for two reasons:

1. to see what filed items still remain to be acted upon or to add additional items for filing
2. to reinforce and ensure retention and accessibility. The occasional mental review is this reinforcement.

If a fact, idea, or thing to do is originally registered vividly, it will usually remain recallable for at least a day or more. This is plenty of time to act on that information, since it is normally mentally filed for action on that particular day. Occasional mental review of your file on the same day ensures recall for that day and probably longer. This is all you have to do. After that, the information will fade out by itself because you don't need it anymore, and you will have discontinued your review of it.

CONTROLLED ERASURE

To deliberately erase a filed item, all you do is use that same cue word to file new information. The new mental picture association immediately takes precedence over the old one, and you will know which the new one is when you review your file. Either the old item will have disappeared or your memory will tell you loudly and clearly which item is most recent.

Another way you may be able to erase your previous mental picture is by visualizing a particular cue word as being clear and empty. Just see that file place without anything else pictured with it. In this way you can deliberately clear the file. I prefer the first method, in which you merely re-record over the same tape. This is a one-step operation that clears the file of previous information and adds new material at the same time.

THE NUMBER-RHYME FILE

Another useful file, and one that has had some popularity, is the Number-Rhyme System. Each number has a rhyming cue word that not only retrieves a filed item, but automatically tells you its numerical position as well. Whenever this last feature is important or desirable, this is the file system to use. You can either use the following rhyming cues or make up your own.

   1:   Bun
   2:   Glue
   3:   Tree
   4:   Door
   5:   Dive (See yourself diving into a pool)
   6:   Bricks
   7:   Heaven
   8:   Gate
   9:   Wine
  10:   Tent
  11:   Elephant
  12:   Shelf

Number ten could, of course, be rhymed with Hen, or Den, for a better rhyme, if you like. Note that from number eleven on, the rhymes are imperfect. Nevertheless, they will work if your pictures for them are vivid. Some of these numbers could be "rhymed" as follows:

13: Flirting
14: Courting
15: Lifting
16: Mixed Teens
17: Heaven Seen
18: Made Team
19: Winding
20: Plenty

The fact that the rhyme words after ten are not all concrete picturable nouns makes them more difficult to picture. That is why this number-rhyme code is usually used for about ten or twelve items only.

There are other ways to extend the number-rhyme system beyond the original ten, but they are somewhat cumbersome and tend to defeat the system's essential simplicity, so they will not be mentioned here. If you find that you need a system beyond ten or twelve cues that also tell you the *position* of the item in your list, the ABC file fills the need.

THE *ABC* RHYME FILE

The alphabet has twenty-six letters, and the ABC file therefore has twenty-six cue words, all in rhyme. This system works exactly the same as the others. Here are the twenty-six letters and their cues:

A: = *A*pe
B: = *Bee*
C: = *Sea*
D: = *Deed*
E: = *Eel*
F: = *Ef*fort (see a
       weightlifter)
G: = *G*-string
H: = *H*-bomb
I: = *I*ce

J: = *J*ay (blue jay)
K: = *K*-9 (security dog)
L: = *El*evator
M: = *Em*pire State
       Building
N: = *En*gine
O: = *O*pal, *O*boe, or *O*wl
P: = *Pea*
Q: = *Cue* (billiard cue) or
       *C*ucumber

R: = A*r*m   W: = *Double-hue*
S: = *Es*kimo   (rainbow)
T: = *Tee* (golf)   X: = *X*-ray
U: = *U*ke (ukulele) or   Y: = *Y*MCA (gym)
       U-boat   Z: = *Z*ebra
V: = *V*enus

As said before, you can use whatever words seem best to you as long as they rhyme and are easily picturable. Once you select an alphabetical cue word, however, you should stick with it to avoid confusion.

NUMBERS AND LETTERS TOGETHER

If you park your car in a spot designated 9B, and you want to memorize this, you can use a combination of the number-rhyme file and the ABC rhyme file. Just picture a glass of red *wine* (9), with a *bee* (B) swimming in it, on your dashboard. If the parking lot location (or whatever it is) is marked, say, 35-J, you might picture a *tree* (3) making a *dive* (5) at a blue *jay* (J) and scaring it off. Or, using the Number-Meaning Method from Chapter 4, simply picture a quarter and a dime (35) being pecked at by a jay (J). If you think you can remember these simple number-and-letter combinations without such picturing, then by all means do so. Or write them down, if you prefer. But if you have no pencil or paper, or if you forget your car location, I guarantee that you will wish you had reinforced that car location with a memory aid! That's what they're for, and that's why you're learning them. These aids constitute substantial memory insurance when you need it.

To remember a long number that also includes alphabetical letters—serial numbers, ID numbers, credit card numbers, etc.—use the Number-Meaning Method from the chapter on numbers, and just insert the proper ABC file cue picture for the letter or letters involved.

A PERSONALIZED MEMORY MEMENTO

As far as I know, this is an original idea. It is a very nice personalized little gift you can give to someone—a custom-made Mental Filing System based on the letters of his or her name.

For example, your friend's name is ALICE SMYTH. If you take a piece of paper and write down the letters of her name in a vertical column, including your ABC cue word for each letter, you would come up with this:

A: *A*pe
L: *El*evator
I: *I*ce
C: *Sea*
E: *E*el
S: *Es*kimo
M: *Em*pire State Building
Y: *Y*MCA
T: *Tee*
H: *H*-Bomb

Now, all you have to do is teach Alice Smyth how to use it and explain how it can help her remember the important things she wants to do. Demonstrate it or have her try it herself to make sure she understands the simple procedure. Then give her this piece of paper, her personalized memory system, as a souvenir. At the very least, this will be the most unusual and useful little memento your friend or business acquaintance ever received, and there is little doubt that he or she will always remember you for it.

For business use, you can use your calling card and personalize the ABC file for a customer or client on the back of it, over lunch or dinner, complete with a little lesson and demonstration. You will be surprised at the impression you create, especially if the person is perceptive enough to appreciate such an unusual little personal reminder system.

If certain letters in the person's name are repeated, this is no problem. Just use such repeated letters only once, the first time they appear. If the name is very short, ask for the middle name and include it in the system. If the name is still too short, add a Mr., Mrs., Miss, or Ms., as appropriate.

If your work involves meeting people, this little idea can be worth many times the price of this book to you, and at this writing you can be certain that you are the only one who is likely to give such a novel and useful remembrance.

THE BRAIN CHAIN MENTAL FILE

Early in the book you used the Brain Chain to memorize and recall a list of twelve unrelated words or items. Instead of using a preset sequence of memorized file cues, you simply took each new item of information and pictorially associated it with the next, linking them as you went along.

An important characteristic of the Brain Chain is that each chain you form is a self-contained unit. New information is not refiled with it, as in the other mental filing systems. Each Brain Chain you form holds only its own particular information. If this Brain Chain is reinforced with occasional use, it becomes a permanent possession and the information it holds is always accessible to you. Do not overlook this little-realized fact about the Brain Chain. It is valuable; with it, you can have an unlimited number of such chains of permanently remembered facts and ideas at your constant command for a lifetime.

The body file, house file, number rhyme file, and ABC file are all erasable and can be filled with new information continuously. For this reason they are most often used for the filing of temporarily needed information.

FINAL THOUGHTS ON MENTAL FILING

It has been said that the greatest natural time-saver known to man is a reliable memory. Even so, the concept of mental filing is foreign to most people. They may have heard the term, but actual use of the system remains outside their experience. I hope that by now you can perceive the practical value of such a systematic reminder file.

Overall, mental filing systems fulfill two basic needs:

Temporary Remembering:

1. for things to be done, daily priorities
2. facts and information to know and use, but which need not be remembered permanently

Permanent Remembering:

1. Any information committed to memory with a mental filing system can be remembered permanently through purposeful, periodic mental reviews of such filed information.

The mental filing systems taught in this chapter are as follows:

1. The Body File
2. The House File
3. The Number-Rhyme File
4. The ABC File

We also reviewed the importance of the Brain Chain as a mental file for permanent chains of knowledge. (The Brain Chain can be reviewed in Chapter 2.)

The Memory Control techniques used in mental filing are contained in the acronym PAR.

P = PICTURE IT
A = ASSOCIATE IT
R = REVIEW IT

PAR is a useful reminder and formula for better remembering in general. It is also a description of retrieval cues and their function:

Pay **A**ttention and **R**emember
with
Positive **A**ction **R**eminders
for
Power **A**ssisted **R**ecall

THE DIFFERENCE BETWEEN
EFFICIENCY AND EFFECTIVENESS

Efficiency is doing things right.
Effectiveness is doing the right things.

Used properly, these mental filing systems will enable you to do the right right things. There is an old saying:

People remember 10 percent of what they hear.
25 percent of what they see and hear.
And 90 percent of what they *do*.

With this in mind, I urge you to learn and use the mental filing systems best suited for your particular needs. They will make your everyday working memory far more reliable than it is now. You will have a powerful, accurate, easy, fast, built-in reminder system that works twenty-four hours a day.

10

A Working Memory
for Special Purposes

Now that you have learned some basic memory management
techniques, you can begin to apply them to many practical
situations that may have given you trouble before. You may
have wished that you could deliver a speech without notes, or
remember important facts about people besides their names.
You may have forgotten the meaning of a particular word or
would like to increase your vocabulary more quickly. Perhaps
you have wished for an easier way to learn a foreign language.
You may need a more efficient and dependable way of studying
and retaining what you read. Perhaps you are a harried executive who worries about "losing your touch" because you cannot
seem to remember the constant stream of moment-to-moment
details and all the priorities that keep coming up. You may be a
sales representative who realizes that good memory is good
business, but have difficulty remembering the spoken word in
situations where taking notes is inconvenient or taboo. We will
now cover these and other special-purpose situations in which
the techniques you learned can be used.

MENTALLY RECORDING ON-THE-SPOT CONFIDENTIAL INFORMATION

Recently I gave a Memory Effectiveness Seminar for a large industrial firm. A day or two before the program, the national sales manager asked me if I could teach their sales representatives to memorize spoken information so that the speaker (the client or customer) would not be aware of such memorization. It was explained to me that often during a sales interview a client reveals confidential information about his company, his company's needs, specific details about competitors, company pricing policies, product availability, and other such information that cannot be written down. Such information is not for publication. However, upon hearing such information, the sales representative is instantly aware of its present and future importance to him and his company. Common sense tells him that such unexpected revelations can be a genuine opportunity for greater profits or, if he forgets these facts, they can mean a genuine loss.

This kind of situation frequently perplexes sales professionals and their managers. Fortunately, an unusual but entirely practical solution for this problem does exist. The answer is to use a Mental Filing System while you are listening to your client or customer. You file the facts as you hear them. Later, when you return to your car, you can recall the pertinent information and make whatever written notes you desire.

Becoming such an expert listener requires practice, but you now have a method to help you. Learning to read or to drive a car also took some effort, but after you mastered it, it was easy. Developing this particular skill also becomes easy if you are willing to give this idea the attention it deserves. If you are a lawyer, therapist, investigator, salesperson, negotiator, or any other practitioner who must remember information without being obvious about it, you will readily see the value of this concept.

Now let's get back to the specific sales situation I described.

Imagine that you are a sales representative with a trained memory who is sitting across the desk from an important buyer. Your product is pianos, and during the conversation the buyer says something like the following:

"I'm going to tell you something confidential. We don't want our competitors to get wind of this, but we've signed a contract to enlarge our main display area, and when it is completed we'll have a lot more room for inventory. Our division manager just might be thinking of adding at least twenty more grand pianos and spinets to the floor. Now, neither you nor your company ever pulled any punches with me, so I'll level with you on something that's not for publication. We recently put out feelers to your biggest competitor, and as a result, they might come across with pianos comparable to yours—at $100 less per unit, *including* benches, plus help in financing our advertising!"

Now, to any piano salesperson's ears, *that* is an earful. It is certainly worth remembering and of great practical interest to you and your company for future strategy and profit. But since this valuable information was presented to you as confidential, you can hardly reach for your pencil.

You instantly decide to use your body file (or whatever other mental file is not filled at the moment) and proceed as follows:

Using the body file for this example, here is what you do: Start with the first thing the buyer mentioned.

Facts to File	**Mental Filing Procedure**
1. "Twenty more pianos."	File it in your *hair*. Put a miniature piano, playing very loudly, in your hair. See it, hear it, feel it, and see a big number 20 branded on the wood, still smoking.
2. "$100 less per piano, by your competitor."	File it in your *nose*. See yourself sneezing, with dozens of $100 bills, each with a thick, black *minus sign* on it, coming out of your nose.

Facts to File	Mental Filing Procedure
3. "including piano bench."	File it with your *mouth*. See yourself biting off the top of a piano bench. Chew it or spit it out and take another bite. It's delicious. Taste and smell the wood and varnish.
4. "plus help in financing our advertising."	File it in your *hands*. Instantly see yourself holding the newspaper, looking at a full page of pianos pictured on sale—by your competitor.

That's it. You have filed the essential points in four chunks, from which you can later reconstruct the story. Keep it very simple and picture only the key facts. The details will fill in themselves for you later on. The piano in your hair with the smoking brand *20* will remind you of the fact that your client may need twenty more pianos. If you think about this for a moment, you will remember that the reason for the extra pianos is that your client's main display room is to be enlarged.

When you later picture your *nose* file, the $100 bills you sneeze out (with minus signs) will bring back to you "$100 *less* per piano by your competitor." When you scan your *mouth* file and see yourself biting off the top of a piano bench you will instantly know that this represents "including the piano bench."

When you scan your *hands* file, you'll see the piano ad in the newspaper, which will remind you that your competitor is offering to help your client with his advertising.

What this amounts to is a technique that forces you to pay attention, listen carefully, and systematically register information, point by point, as you hear it. As such, it is a highly accurate listening and retention device.

Mental filing, as a listening and recording device, can be

applied in other situations when making notes is either imprac-tical or inconvenient. It can be used profitably for remembering important points while listening to a speaker, and especially for following specific directions that may be given only once. At business meetings and conferences, mentally filing pertinent points and then using them effectively in a final review or summation of the meeting is not only a valuable contribution, but an impressive performance to witness as well. Skill in mental filing is the surest way to attain a high degree of reliability and accuracy in remembering what you hear. The person who can mentally file and recall the right information at the right time has a practical and priceless asset that few can equal.

SPEAKING WITHOUT NOTES

The Planned Speech

First, in order to speak without notes, you must know your subject thoroughly. Beyond this, what you need is a series of mental reminders of each key point or section in the proper order. Specifically, you must first organize your speech, get it down on paper. When you have the format laid out, you are ready to connect each key point with a cue word in your mental file. Use the PAR techniques—picturing, association, and review—exactly as you have been taught.

Once these items are filed, reviewing is very important. Con-tinue reviewing until you can instantly call to mind each key point in the sequence of your speech.

Your next job is to rehearse the speech itself, without looking at notes, until you are so sure of it that if you were awakened at 3:00 A.M. in the middle of a jungle rainstorm, you could instantly run out of your tent and deliver the speech perfectly. Every successful repetition develops your confidence. It is also a good idea to see in advance the room in which you will give the speech. Just becoming familiar with those surroundings will put you more at ease. If at all possible, you might even get up on the platform and either mentally or actually deliver your speech. If you are not an experienced public speaker, this is the best preparation you can have.

To summarize:

1. Know your material thoroughly.
2. Mentally file it and practice recall of the key items to perfection.
3. Rehearse the speech itself until you *know* you can do it effectively.
4. Rehearse it some more!

Always remember the five P's of good speaking: "Proper Preparation Prevents Poor Performance."

The Unprepared Speech

When you are called on to speak unexpectedly, the situation is quite different. You have very little time, if any, to prepare something before you have to stand up in front of the group. There is an old speech formula that is good to keep in mind for such moments. It is called the 3-T Formula:

T = "Tell 'em what you're going to tell 'em."
T = "Tell 'em."
T = "Tell 'em what you told 'em."

This will help you speak with at least a semblance of some form having a beginning, a middle, and an end.

Another, more specific way to organize your speech if you have a little advance notice is to compile a mental list of points you wish to cover and then mentally file them, review them once or twice, and you are ready to rise and speak.

By keeping in mind either of these impromptu speech devices, you can have better assurance of a decent spontaneous speech.

THE *ABC*'s OF REMEMBERING WHAT YOU READ

The more you study, the more you learn.
The more you learn, the more you forget.
The more you forget, the less you know.
Why study?

The only way to be sure of remembering what you read is first to recognize what you want to remember and then to do something about it then and there. There are three effective procedures by which you can "do something about it" while you are reading. Any one, or all three of them in combination, will substantially increase your retention of the information.

Stop, Think, and Review

Stop and think about what you are reading. Mull it over. Compare and contrast the material with things you already know. Talk to yourself about what you want to remember, as you learned to do in Chapter 5. Recite the material to yourself, thereby rehearsing future recall of the material itself. Discuss the material with others. Also remember that the simple repetition of reading the material over for a few times *aloud* permits multisensory registration. You see it, hear it, say it, and think it. Finally, use the material in conversation or at other opportunities, as often as you can. Just remember the TRU Formula for retention:

*T*hink about it; *R*eview it or repeat it; *U*se it.

Studying for Better Remembering

This second approach involves effective study methods that you can find in any good book on study skills. One such widely recommended method is the SQ3R system, which stands for *S*urvey, *Q*uestion, *R*ead, *R*ecite, and *R*eview. As you can see, this method is basically similar to the previous approach, but

SQ3R is a carefully structured, five-step method that extracts the maximum meaning from written material for better understanding and retention.

At this point I also want to call your attention to the ARC method for absorbing written materials, which is explained in Chapter 11.

Reading and Mental Filing

When you want to remember specific facts or materials for a specific purpose such as an exam, a business meeting or conference, or an interview, you can use one of the Mental Filing Systems. Any of them will do the job for you.

The actual method for filing as you read involves choosing key points or facts and either filing them as you read (taking whatever time you need for vivid registration) or listing them first on paper in your order of preference. Then record them in your mental file.

If it is material to be remembered more permanently, the Brain Chain method may be preferable. Remember that you can have as many permanent chains of knowledge as you like. The only requirement is that you forge the links properly in the beginning and then just review the chain from time to time.

The house file can also be used to file things permanently. Some executives in my memory courses have constructed house files of fifty or more file places, and they use them for one, two, or three entirely separate but permanent lists of information. For years I have used similar techniques. I assure you that it works quite dependably. You have only to try these methods for yourself.

REMEMBERING FACTS ABOUT PEOPLE

A good memory for names is a decided asset, but the ability to remember names plus specific facts about people—where they are from, what their interests are, and what kind of work they do—is better. All such information makes people more meaningful in business and social settings. The method is simple, and it fits right in with what you have already learned.

All you have to do is picture the facts you want to remember and add them to the mental picture you have already made for the name and face. Like the name cues and face cues, think of these facts as fact cues. If you meet a Mr. Bloch with red hair, you can visualize *red blocks* in his hair, which will do nicely for the name and face. But if you want to remember that he is with IBM, you can, for example, see white letters on each of those red blocks spelling IBM.

If you meet a Ms. Pierce, who has irregular teeth, and she tells you she is an author, you can see her biting a chunk out of her new novel. She *pierces* it with her teeth. Reinforce this image by thinking, "Pierce is fierce. She eats her own books!" This image and thought are striking enough to remind you later on that she is an author.

Here are a few more examples of name and fact connections.

Name	Occupation	Conversions and Connections
MacKenzie	gardener	See a *Mack* truck going through a *garden*.
Beecher	physician	On the *beach* is the doctor's office. Get examined and take a dive.
Allie	salesman	Muhammad *Ali* is trying to *sell* you boxing gloves.
Gumm	typist	See a typewriter full of gum.
Iver	TV repair man	Iver's *ivy* is climbing all over his TV screen.
Holmes	banker	Holmes's *home* is owned by the bank. Piggy bank. You can bank on it. (repetition-reinforcement)
Kingston	commercial artist	As an artist, Kingston draws only *kings, stun*ningly. Stunning Kings by Kingston.

Name	Occupation	Conversions and Connections
Garzon	dog trainer	(Garzon-Carson) See Garzon with Carson on television, training a dog.
Jerry Fenter	athlete from Brooklyn	See a *cherry* on a *fender*; it falls off into a *brook* and swims like an *athlete*.
Bea Fielding	singer from Texas	See *bees* in a *field, singing*, as they attack *cowboy hats*. (Texas)

Remember that the purpose of this procedure is not to make your mental picturing either logical or illogical but to make it *memorable*. All that counts is that the means or method you use produces dependable recall.

ENGLISH VOCABULARY

Learning New Words with the CCR System

Learning new words to increase your vocabulary is always a worthwhile activity. However, looking words up in the dictionary is no guarantee that you will remember their meanings. A dictionary is like a school; it gives the facts but doesn't show how to remember them. You can overcome this by using the CCR (Convert, Connect, Review) System that you learned for remembering names and faces.

Take the word *perquisite*, for example. It means benefits or privileges over and above the usual. If *perquisite* is meaningless to you at the moment, it has the same effect on you as hearing a meaningless name for the first time. Therefore, the first thing to do is to convert that word (as you would a name) into something that sounds or looks like that word. Two such words that occur to me are *perk* and *exquisite*. After we so convert, we must *connect*; simply tie the words *perk* and *exquisite* into a thought or sentence containing the meaning of the word *perquisite*. The first sentence that occurs to me is: "*Perk* up for your *exquisite* benefits and bonuses."

We have now associated perquisite with perk, exquisite, benefits and bonuses. The sentence makes the meaning of perquisite clear, so you now review by simply saying the sentence once or twice to let it sink in. The best review, of course, is using your new word as soon as you can in conversation. Use is the best reinforcement for retention.

Let's take another word, *pernicious*. It means ruinous, hurtful, injurious, or wicked. The name Fern rhymes with the first part of the word, *pern*, and the word *vicious* rhymes with the last part of per*nicious*. With this in mind, you can easily think of the sentence, "Fern is vicious and pernicious." Of course, not all words lend themselves to such close rhyming, but very many do, and if you can think of such similar-sounding words, the job of understanding and remembering is made much easier for you.

Similar-sounding words (or parts of words, like *perk* and *perq*uisite) do not have to be rhymes in order to work. Any word or phrase you think of that sounds or looks like the new vocabulary word will do the trick. These similar elements are retrieval cues, which effectively remind you of the new word and its meaning.

A few more examples of the CCR method applied to new words are in the table on page 166.

Review of the Method

Convert: To learn a new vocabulary word in English, think of another word that sounds or looks like the new word or that is similar to at least a main part of the new word.

Connect: Then form a short phrase or sentence including the similar sound or look-alike word or words with the meaning of the new word and, if possible, the new word itself. It is important to picture this interaction vividly.

Word to Learn	Similar Sound or Look-Alike Conversion	Definition	Memory Phrase Connection
sibilant	Sybil's aunt	The hissing sound, "sssssssssss"	*Sybil's aunt* hisses, Sssssss!
mendacious	men, gracious	false, untrue, a lie, dishonest	*Men* who are *gracious* are not mendacious; they tell the truth!
peregrination	bear, grin, nation	to travel or journey, especially on foot	*Bear* and *grin* it as you walk the *nation*. or *Perry grins* as he walks the *nation*.
jocosity	Joe cuss city	joking or jesting	*Joe cussed* our *city* jokingly.
salubrious	salute to us	healthful	A *salute* to *us* and health.
grampus	grandpa	a large fish	*Grandpa* is a big fish.
calumniate	column eight	to make false and malicious statements	*Column eight* is false and malicious.

Review: Say the phrase or sentence a few times, then use the new word in conversation as soon as you can and as often as appropriate in order to incorporate it into your permanent vocabulary and to keep it accessible to recall.

FOREIGN LANGUAGE VOCABULARY

Learning words in foreign languages is facilitated by the exact CCR method we used above. A strange foreign word is no different from a strange word in English. Either one is a meaningless sequence of letters until you attach meaning to it. Here is the CCR System again, applied to learning words in other languages.

To learn foreign words, first be sure you know the correct pronunciation and meaning. Then proceed as follows:

Convert: As before, try to think of a similar-sounding or similar-looking word (or short phrase) in English.

Connect: Associate this word or phrase to the foreign word's meaning, expressed in a phrase or sentence. Mentally picture this interaction as vividly as you can while you repeat the phrase or sentence.

Review: Use the new word as often as is appropriate in order to plant it firmly and keep it accessible.

The tables on the following pages will show you how to use the system for learning words in French, Spanish, Italian, and German.

CALENDAR INFORMATION

Remembering Which Months Have 30/31 Days

There is a faster way to know the number of days in a particular month than by dutifully recalling,

FRENCH

Word to Learn and Pronunciation	Similar-Sound or Look-Alike Word in English Conversion	English Translation	Memory Phrase Connection
eau (oh!)	Oh!	water	Oh! I want some water.
livre (lee-vra)	libra (sign of zodiac)	book	Libra is in the book.
usine (u-zeen)	using	factory	Using the factory is productive.
drapeau (drah-poe)	drop old	flag	Drop old flags.
stylo (steelo)	steal old	pen	Steal old pens.
dind (dand)	Dan (a first name)	turkey	Dan is a dandy turkey.

	Similar-Sound or Look-Alike Word in English Conversion	English Translation	Memory Phrase Connection
ecrire (ay-creer)	career	to write	A *career* in *writing*.
sur (soor)	sir	over	*Sir*, it's all *over*!
négliger (neg-lee-zhai)	negligee	overlook	The *negligee* was *overlooked*.

SPANISH

Word to Learn and Pronunciation	Similar-Sound or Look-Alike Word in English Conversion	English Translation	Memory Phrase Connection
caro (cah-roe)	car, oh!	expensive	That *car, oh*, how *expensive*!
gripe (gree-pay)	agree to pay	flu	I *agree to pay* for a *flu* shot.

SPANISH

Word to Learn and Pronunciation	Similar-Sound or Look-Alike Word in English Conversion	English Translation	Memory Phrase Connection
duro (doo-ro)	to row	hard	*To row is hard.*
campo (cahm-po)	calm pole	field	*A calm Pole is in the field.*
ojo (oh-ho)	Oh-ho!	eye	*Oh-ho! You touched my eye.*
hoy (oi)	toy	today	*Buy a toy today.*
comida (co-mee-da)	go meet her	dinner	*Go meet her for dinner.*
charco (char-co)	charcoal	puddle	*The charcoal fell in the puddle.*

tonto (ton-toe)	Tonto (Indian friend of Lone Ranger)	fool	*Tonto* was a *fool.*

ITALIAN

Word to Learn and Pronunciation	Similar-Sound or Look-Alike Word in English Conversion	English Translation	Memory Phrase Connection
poco (po-co)	poke	little	*Poke* him a *little.*
forte (for-tay)	Fort "A"	loud	*Fort "A"* had a *loud* explosion.
giovane (joe-vahn)	Joe wants	young	*Joe wants* to be *young.*

ITALIAN

Word to Learn and Pronunciation	Similar-Sound or Look-Alike Word in English Conversion	English Translation	Memory Phrase Connection
apertura (ah-per-tiu-ra)	aperture	opening	The *aperture* is *opening*.
cappa (cah-pah)	copper	cloak	The *copper* wore a *cloak*.
mento (men-toe)	meant to	chin	I *meant to* *chin* myself.
sereno (sehr-en-o)	serene	cloudless	The sky was *serene* and *cloudless*.
freddo (fred-do)	Alfredo	cold	*Alfredo* is *cold*.
rapido (ra-pee-do)	repeat "Oh"	fast, quick	*Repeat "Oh"* *quickly*.

GERMAN

Word to Learn and Pronunciation	Similar-Sound or Look-Alike Word in English Conversion	English Translation	Memory Phrase Connection
bitten (bit-ten)	bitten	request	He was *bitten* by *request!*
band (bond)	bond	ribbon	The *bond* was made by a *ribbon.*
befriedigen (be-freed-i-gen)	be freed again	satisfy	To *be freed again* is most *satisfying.*
untertasse (oon-ter-ta-sai)	under Tessie	saucer	*Under Tessie* lies the *saucer.*
schere (sha-ra)	share the	scissors	Please *share the scissors.*
etwas (et-vas)	it was	something	*It was* really *something!*

GERMAN

Word to Learn and Pronunciation	Similar-Sound or Look-Alike Word in English Conversion	English Translation	Memory Phrase Connection
fleck (flek)	flick	spot, stain	*Flick* the *spot* to remove the *stain*.
muster (moos-ter)	rooster	specimen	That *rooster* is a fine *specimen*.
essen (es-sen)	essence	food	The *essence* of life is *food*.

"Thirty days hath September
April, June, and November
All the rest have thirty-one
Except February, which has 28
And in leap year 29."

All you have to do is to memorize, once and for all, this simple four-word phrase: June April's Novel, September. (NOVEL stands for NOVEMBER.) In this way, by merely thinking of an author (*June April*) and her new *novel, September*, you instantly know all the months with thirty days. If the month in question is not one of these, you know instantly that it has thirty-one days. The only exception is February, and you already know, without help, that it has twenty-eight or twenty-nine days.

The Fingertip System

Here is another tried and true method of remembering the number of days in any month. Follow this simple procedure:

1. Hold out your left hand, palm up, and bend your thumb into your palm.
2. At this point your four left fingers should be extended and held apart. Now, with the tip of your right forefinger, touch the top joint (finger pad) of your left index finger. Now move your right finger to the right, and it will drop into the space between your left first and second fingers. Continue to touch each left finger and the space in the same way, as follows: finger 2, space, finger 3, space, finger 4. All you have to know is this: Each finger you touch is a month with thirty-one days. Each space you touch is a month with thirty days or fewer.
    You always do it from left to right, in order, as follows:

FINGER 1	(SPACE)	
January	February	
(31 days)	(28)	
FINGER 2	(SPACE)	
March	April	
(31)	(30)	
FINGER 3	(SPACE)	FINGER 4
May	June	July
(31)	(30)	(31)

Now, merely start over again, touching your left forefinger again, continuing from left to right, and naming the succeeding months as follows:

FINGER 1	(SPACE)	
August	September	
FINGER 2	(SPACE)	FINGER 3
October	November	December

Remembering Birthdays, Anniversaries, Appointments

By using the Number-Meaning Method combined with a person's name, you can mentally file the information for use in the near future. For example, let's say you want to remember the following friends and dates:

The Oakleys: anniversary, November 3.
Joe: birthday, April 9.
Margaret: birthday, December 30.
Jack Mackelroy: appointment, Monday at 4:00 P.M.

All you really do is create retrieval cues based on the name and date in the form of mental pictures and/or a phrase or sentence. The following are some ways to do this. Many more can be created depending on your imagination and creativity.

For the Oakleys, first you give the name a little more meaning so that you can picture it: an oak tree, for instance. The same goes for their anniversary date, November 3. It needs some picturable meaning. November is Thanksgiving, so why not use a *turkey* to symbolize November in your mind? As for the date, number *3*, just rhyme it with free, and you have a free turkey, which quickly symbolizes November 3. Now, in order to put it all in order, you can mentally see the Oakleys climbing an oak tree to grab a free turkey. (The turkey has a "FREE" sign hanging on it.) You can also reinforce this by thinking of this sentence: "The Oakleys climb an *oak tree* to get a *free turkey*. Just say it a few times to yourself as you picture it, and the name Oakley will recall the anniversary date for you by pure association.

Now for Joe's birthday on April 9th. If you know a girl or woman named April, see Joe holding hands with her as they both drink wine (rhymes with 9). Or you can simply picture Joe dramatically turning into an ape (April) and drinking wine. To reinforce this, say or think to yourself, "When Joe loses his temper, he turns into an *ape* and has to drink *wine* to calm down." There you have it: Joe and April 9.

Next is Margaret's birthday, December 30. Just picture Margaret hugging a Santa Claus (December), who is dirty (30). Reinforce it by simply repeating to yourself a couple of times, "Who would ever know that *Margaret* has a secret passion for a *dirty Santa*?"

You can remember appointments in the same way. Suppose you have an appointment with Jack Mackelroy at 4:00 P.M. on Monday. Just visualize him opening the closet door (4), and money (Monday) falls to the floor (4 again). See the bills and coins shower to the floor. "*Mackelroy* opens the *door* and *money* falls to the *floor*."

See how simple it is? Yes, it does take some imagination, but remember that if you want to remember, you must do something about it. Being creative is fun, and it works. If you want to remember that Mackelroy's birthday is, say, March 25, you might set it up this way: Just think to yourself, "Mackelroy *marches*, because he has *plenty* of *drive* (Plenty, drive = twenty-five, rhymed). The rhyme remembers. Take advantage of this valuable fact and let it work for you.

If you're wondering how to picture each weekday to remember appointments, such as *money* for Monday, or how to picture each of the twelve months, here are some ways to do it simply and effectively. Remember that you can use anything that you think of that is easy for you. If you create the method, it will work even better.

Weekday Picture Symbols

Monday: Money, moon

Tuesday: *Newsday* (newspaper)

Wednesday: Men's day (see men)

Thursday: Nurse day (a nurse)

Friday: Fry day (frying pan)

Saturday: Saturn (planet with rings)

Sunday: The sun, a sundae

Monthly Picture Symbols

January: *Jan*itor

February: *Web* or *Fob*

March: March, margarine, Marge

April: Ape, showers (April showers)

May: Maid, maiden

June: Bride (June bride), juice

July: July 4 (fireworks), jewel

August: Auburn (color), auction, au gratin, au jus

September: Scepter, timber

October: Octopus

November: Turkey, no member, ember

Weekday Picture Symbols   **Monthly Picture Symbols**

December: Santa, Christmas tree

Remembering Noteworthy Dates and Events

There is another effective way to handle memory for dates and events. Instead of coding each month with a picture symbol (January, janitor; April, showers; May, maid; etc.), you can simply use number meaning and/or rhymes for those numbers. For example, instead of "December" 1, think of it as 12/1, or "a dozen and one." Thus, if you wanted to remember Woody Allen's birthday, 12/1/35, you could code it with this sentence:

12/   1/   35

Woody Allen told a *dozen and one dirty lies*! (*Dirty lies* roughly rhymes with thirty-five.)

Here are a few more celebrities and their birthdates, coded with sentencing.

> *Babe Ruth to fix nine wives.* (2/6/95)
> *Arthur Rubinstein* has *one* piano *28* inches high, with *87* keys. (1/28/87)
> *Red Buttons* is *new* and *live* for *one-night*ers. (2/5/19)
> *Meryl Streep's sex boo-boo* was a *nifty one.* (6/22/51)
> *Bob Hope* is *free tonight. Oh, gee!* (3/29/03)
> *Orson Welles* does *three tricks* in *fifteen* minutes. (3/6/15)
> *Elke Sommers's eleph*ant *flies* into *door one.* (11/5/41)
> *Luciano Pavarotti* sings with *ten dozen dirty flies.* (10/12/35)

With these methods, you convert names and numbers—dates, anniversaries, events, appointments, etc.—into meaningful symbols (monthly picture symbols and/or number-rhyme phrases or sentences) for easy registration and retrieval. All you have to do is say the coded sentence a few times to register it initially.

REMEMBERING JOKES
(A SHORT COURSE FOR SHORT MEMORIES)

Millions of people bemoan the fact that they can't remember jokes. "As soon as I hear a good one, it's gone," is a familiar refrain. Most memory books teach ways to remember jokes and stories by mentally coding punch lines or organizing jokes by categories and developing written files. This is all fine, except that in reality the only people who take the time and trouble to use such methods are professional comedians and speakers. It's their stock in trade. Even so, the only way they keep the material accessible to memory is by actually using the material.

If this applies to the professionals, it applies even more so to the nonprofessional, occasional joke teller. So I am not going to give you any unrealistic methods and systems for remembering jokes. All you need to know is the following sentence:

The best way to remember jokes is simply to retell them in your own words as soon after you hear the jokes as possible.

After this, an occasional retelling is usually all that is necessary to keep them accessible.

There is one particular joke that has always intrigued me because of its natural associative flow. It is probably one of the easiest jokes of all to learn and remember. If you start it right, you can hardly go wrong. It's an old one, but a good one. If possible, read it aloud a few times, and once you feel the natural flow of the thing you'll have at least one good joke you'll be sure to remember. This joke works by pure association all the way through. One thing leads to another. Once you say it a few times, I think you'll find it more difficult to forget than it is to learn. Here it is.

There are only two things you have to worry about:
Whether you're healthy or whether you're sick.
If you're healthy, you have nothing to worry about.
If you're sick, you have two things to worry about:
Whether you live or whether you die.
If you live, you have nothing to worry about.
If you die, you have two things to worry about:
Whether you go to heaven, or whether you go to hell.
If you go to heaven, you have nothing to worry about.
If you go to hell, you'll be so busy shaking hands with all your friends
that you won't have *time* to worry anymore!

As soon as the natural associative flow gains momentum in this particular joke, you will find that it almost "tells itself." After you read it a couple of times, tell it in your own words, and it will be just as effective.

MAKING FACTS EASIER TO REMEMBER

First-Letter Mnemonics

Many times you can take information and arrange it in such a way that it is not only easier to remember but actually difficult to forget. One of my former seminar students, an engineer, calls this the MIETR principle:

*M*ake *I*t *E*asier *T*o *R*emember

First-letter mnemonics (acronyms and acrostics) can make many facts much easier to remember. They are quick, miniature filing systems that tenaciously hold information in mind. They appear everywhere and are condensations of whatever it is that they represent. Here are examples of first-letter mnemonics:

Acronyms

ASAP   (*a*s *s*oon *a*s *p*ossible)

Acronyms

ZIP	(Zone Improvement Program) (Zip codes)
MOUSE	(Minimal Orbital Unmanned Satellite of Earth)
IRAC	(Issue, Rule, Application, and Conclusion) (Law)
PEN	(Plautus, Ennius, and Naevius) (Earliest Roman poets)
ERA	(Equal Rights Amendment)
SAC	(Strategic Air Command)
NOW	(National Organization for Women)
CORE	(Congress Of Racial Equality)

As you can see, an acronym is a pronounceable word, each letter of which represents another word.

Acrostics

An acrostic is a succession of words or lines in which the first letter of each is an item or word to be remembered. Examples:

*E*very *G*ood *B*oy *D*oes *F*ine (5 lines of treble clef music staff, or E G B D F)

*G*reat *B*ig *D*addy (G B D: the first 3 spaces above music staff)

*G*ood *B*oys *D*on't *F*ool *A*round (G B D F A: 5 lines of bass clef music staff)

Another type of related mnemonic, which I call the successive syllable mnemonic, is formed when each syllable or partial syllable of the mnemonic word forms or helps to form a word to be remembered.

Examples: NABISCO (*NA*tional *BIS*cuit *CO*mpany)
GESTAPO (*GE*rman *STA*te *PO*lice)

To sum up first-letter mnemonics, acronyms and acrostics make words or phrases based on the first letters of the items to be remembered. The reason they make things easier to remember is that they make the items more meaningful. In educator's jargon, first-letter mnemonics change a *recall task* into an *aided recall task* by providing retrieval cues to help you recall those items. Research studies show that first-letter mnemonics can significantly improve recall for lists of items.*

DO-IT-YOURSELF MNEMONICS

You can remember useful everyday information with much more assurance if you take a moment or two to invent your own mnemonic. With an acronym, acrostic, rhyme, or other technique you have learned you can say the desired information once or twice to yourself and successfully retain and recall that information thereafter. These mental holding devices hold the information in formation for you, with very little effort and great savings in learning time.

Recently we had to take the car in for a checkup. The radio was full of static, the air conditioner was not working right, and there was a wind noise despite closed windows. We happened to mention these things to our daughter, and she instantly came up with the mnemonic WAR.

W = Windows
A = Air conditioner
R = Radio

Needless to say, we had no trouble at all recalling what had to be checked when we arrived the next day for car service. We

---

* D.L. Nelson and C.S. Archer, "The First-Letter Mnemonic," *Journal of Educational Psychology* 63 (1972):482-86.

didn't even have to try to remember. We all knew it instantly and declared WAR on the service attendant.

If you are driving to the supermarket, and you can't write down the items you are listing mentally as you drive, try the following technique if your mental shopping list is not too long. If it occurs to you, for example, that you need to buy *s*ugar, *n*oodles, *a*pples, and *p*eas, just think of the first letter of each of these items in sequence, and you come up with the word SNAP. If these items occur to you in a different sequence, such as peas, apples, noodles, and sugar, your mnemonic would be PANS. You can rearrange the sequence of items, of course, in any way you like to come up with a suitable reminder word. For instance, in this case, other acronyms might be SPAN or NAPS. The whole idea is just to *observe* the spelling of the items in your mind's eye and invent your own do-it-yourself mnemonic. Then just say the mnemonic to yourself once or twice, and you have a mentally filed shopping list! When you park in the supermarket lot, you can write the items down, if you wish, adding any additional items to your list as desired.

Another way to file shopping items mentally, which you might like even better, could work as follows. Suppose you are driving, and the items that pop into mind for you to buy are noodles, sugar, apples, and peas, as before. Instead of using just the first letter of each item as a reminder, use the first *part* of the word—or the whole word, if possible—and create a simple sentence such as:

(noodles)	(sugar)	(apples)	(peas)
The *new*	sugar	*app*ears	*peace*ful!

Obviously, *new* recalls *noodles*, *sugar* is itself, *app* recalls *apples*, and *peace* recalls *peas*. With such powerful reminders, it would be difficult to *forget* the list.

Another example: If your mental shopping list is formed in this sequence—milk, eggs, lettuce, ice cream, and paper towels—you might easily come up with one of the following mnemonics.

1. MELIP: This first-letter mnemonic is an acronym. Each letter represents its item. You can also mentally rearrange those four items in other sequences, and come up with LIP ME, PILE 'EM, or P. M. ELI, etc. Any of these will do an admirable job of reminding you of the specific items.

2. (lettuce) (ice cream) (paper towels)   (milk)   (eggs)
   Let us   *cream*   *up the towels* with *milk* and *eggs.*

3. (milk)   (eggs)   (ice cream)   (lettuce)   (paper towels)
   *Mil*dred b*egs* for *ice cream*, so *let us* throw in the *towel.*

As you can see, this method of "sentencing" is similar to the sentencing technique in the Number-Meaning Method in Chapter 4.

Not long ago I did a memory training seminar for one of the country's largest industrial salt companies. I usually request information in advance about the company's products and sales and marketing procedures so that I can personalize my presentation to make it more interesting. As I looked over some of the company literature, I noticed its four main methods of salt production and its five major markets. The four methods of salt production were *S*olar Evaporation, *P*an Production, *V*acuum, and *R*ock Salt production. Observing the first letter of each of these four methods, I rearranged them and came up with RSVP. This simple RSVP mnemonic enabled me to put on mental hold those four salt production methods in very short order. I will tell you how I used it in a moment.

The company's five major markets were the fields of *A*griculture, *W*ater Conditioning, *I*ndustry, *F*ood Processing, and *T*ransportation. Once more, I rearranged these five items, and they formed the easy mnemonic TAWFI (toffee). It could have been I. W. FAT, FITAW, WAT IF, WATFI, or others, but TAWFI stuck with me because I love the taste of toffee.

With these two workable mnemonics in mind (RSVP and TAWFI), and after quickly reviewing what they meant, I was easily able to recall the company's four salt production methods and its five major markets at appropriate points in my memory presentation. It goes without saying that this helped make my program more relevant and interesting for this particular group. During the intermission, company managers and executives expressed appreciation for "all the time I must have spent" in learning so much about the company's operations.

MORE USEFUL MEMORY AIDS IN VARIOUS FIELDS

Chapter 6 offers a potpourri of mnemonic reminders of various kinds. Here are a few more that have stood the test of time, plus a few of my own.

The International Electrical Color Code:

This is the color code adopted for numbering resistors and capacitors, worldwide. The colors in correct order are: *B*lack, *B*rown, *R*ed, *O*range, *Y*ellow, *G*reen, *B*lue, *V*iolet, *G*ray, and *W*hite.

The well-known first-letter mnemonic sentence for this sequence is: "*B*ad *B*oys *R*uin *O*ur *Y*oung *G*irls, *B*ut *V*iolet *G*ives *W*illingly."

Zoology

The order of classification in the animal kingdom is *K*ingdom, *P*hylum, *C*lass, *O*rder, *F*amily, *G*enus, *S*pecies, and *V*ariety. A sentence mnemonic for this is: "*K*ings *P*lay *C*hess *O*n *F*ancy *G*reen *S*oft *V*elvet."

Energy

The forms of energy are: *M*echanical, *C*hemical, *S*olar, *H*eat, *A*tomic, *L*ight, and *E*lectrical.

The following three mnemonics occur to me during this writing:

1. *M*ust *C*hemical *S*mog *H*eat *A*dam's *L*ive *E*lectra?
2. Mc SHALE
3. CLASH 'EM! (acronym with changed sequence of energy forms listed)

Law

For a recent seminar I gave for Illinois lawyers, the following mnemonics were created in advance to illustrate strategies for remembering facts in regard to cases, doctrines, and other legal information.

The *Exclusionary Rule Doctrine* resulted from the Supreme Court's decision in the famous *U.S. versus Weeks case.* *Mnemonic:* It took the *U.S. weeks* to *exclude* this case.

Another famous Supreme Court decision resulted in the *Judicial Review Doctrine,* which gives the high court the right to review acts of Congress. That famous case was *Marberry versus Madison. Mnemonic: Marred berries* from *Madison* were *judicially reviewed* by *Congress.*

As you can see, both the case name and the resulting legal doctrine are combined in the makeup of these sentence reminders.

Abnormal Psychology

The four varieties of schizophrenia are: *S*imple, *P*aranoid, *H*ebephrenic, and *C*atatonic. *Mnemonic: S*ad *P*eople—*H*elpful *C*linic; or *S*imple *P*aranoids *H*eat *C*ats.

Geology

Eras: *P*re-Cambrian, *P*aleozoic, *M*esozoic, and *C*enozoic. *Mnemonic: P*lease *P*ass *M*y *C*ave; or *P*reach, *pal*—*mes*sage *cen*sored!

It may have occurred to you that these mnemonics can be very useful in school or college but do not seem useful for more practical, everyday learning and remembering. If this has crossed your mind, remember that the *point* of these mnemonic examples is to show you how they are created, how they work, and how they are used, so that you can create and use *your own* helpful memory aids *whenever you need them.*

11

External Reminders:
Techniques and Strategies

At bottom, what we have been working with so far is *reminders*. Association, mental pictures, reviews, and all the individual techniques and organized systems are actually powerful reminders that trigger your memory's performance. Until now, the types of reminders we have used and created have been internal reminders because they originate in your mind and trigger your memory from within. The Brain Chain, the Number-Meaning Method, the CCR System, and the Mental Filing Systems are all therefore internal reminders.

Virtually all other memory training books and courses to date concentrate only on internal reminders. The few that mention external reminders usually treat them merely as extra things or ideas you might want to know about. External reminders have rarely, if ever, been treated with the attention and respect that they deserve or in sufficient detail and depth.

REMINDERS THAT REMEMBER FOR YOU

Many external reminders trigger your memory so quickly and effortlessly every day of your life that it happens whether or not you are aware of it. Your own surroundings are capable of doing much of your remembering for you. For example, when you notice the ladder you left standing in the middle of the room, you are instantly reminded that you haven't finished painting the ceiling. As you look at that half-painted ceiling, it not only reminds you of the same thing, but it also tells you exactly where to start painting again. If you suddenly hear music coming from your child's room upstairs, you might be reminded to go up and check to see if all homework was completed. Then the telephone rings, and your dentist's receptionist reminds you that you have an appointment tomorrow morning. When you go to get the mail, you see that the monthly bills have arrived, reminding you to pay. You put the mail on your desk in a spot where you will be sure to see it so that you will be reminded again to pay the bills. Later, when you get into your car, the buzzer sounds, reminding you to put on your seat belt or that the door is still open. As you drive, there are signs to remind you of the speed limit. You turn on the car radio, and persuasive voices remind you of sales that are almost over and the money you will save if you buy now. Your turn off your radio, and you look at your gasoline gauge, which reminds you that you need gas. All of these things are effective external reminders that originate in your own environment.

We now come to the key point: *Even when your surroundings seem unable to do any remembering for you, you can deliberately change things so that they will.* Let's take a look at some useful and controllable external memory triggers and how you can use them to your advantage.

SIGHT REMINDERS

The Telephone Reminder

If you have never forgotten to return an important business phone call or make a call that you promised to make, you are an amazing exception. The reminder I'm about to teach works best when you are sitting at your desk with your telephone in sight. Here is how it works: As soon as you tell your caller that you will call back later, or as soon as you form a definite intention to call someone, *take the phone receiver and turn it upside down on the cradle.* It will stay put, even if it looks peculiar. (Remember, it's the out-of-the-ordinary that makes the best reminder.) At the moment you reverse the receiver in the cradle, form a quick but vivid mental image of the person you intend to call *and see him or her sitting on that telephone, pointing a finger at you, demanding, in miniature, that you phone.* You can reinforce the reminder (and your intention) by taking just a second to look straight at the phone and think or say out loud, "Yes, I *will* call you back, so don't glare at me like that."

From then on, every time you notice your upside-down phone you will also see your caller sitting there waiting for you to call back. This in turn will prompt you to make that call when you are ready (or sooner) for two reasons: one, to get rid of your mental image on the phone, and two, to straighten out that receiver!

It doesn't matter how many phone calls you get after you originally reverse the receiver. Just keep reversing it after every such call, until you actually make the return call. Then and only then do you replace the receiver in the cradle the right way.

The Answering Machine Reminder

If you have been forgetting to turn your answering machine on or off, you may be missing important calls. I solved this problem by attaching a neat little sign on the inside of my office door next to the doorknob. On the sign is a small instant camera snapshot of my telephone, plus the two words in big letters, "ON-OFF?" I can't miss it. Every time I leave the office, there it is, looking at me as I reach for the doorknob.

One executive in my seminar informed me later that she had attached a small, attractive piece of metal near her office doorknob. Clinging to it is a circular red magnet one inch in diameter. If her answering machine is on as she leaves the office, she pushes the magnet to the top of the metal piece. If the machine is off, she pushes it to the bottom. Upon leaving her office, the first thing she does is to note the magnet placement, and she responds accordingly then and there.

The Doorknob Reminder

The telephone reminder and the answering machine reminder both use the area just next to a doorknob. Now we will use the doorknob itself as an effective reminder. The idea is simplicity itself, and it couldn't work better.

The next time you think you might forget to take your clothes to the cleaners, put them on a hanger and hang them on the knob of the door you use to leave the house. This is an inescapable reminder. If you use this idea with clothes or anything else you can hang on the doorknob (or put the items on the floor just next to the door or in front of it), there is *no way* you are going to forget that you have to go to the cleaners, mail a letter or package, or return a book to the library.

One day during the memory seminar one of my students, a banker, mentioned that in his house they leave a gold-colored gift wrap string hanging from the front doorknob permanently. Either this string, or a piece of wire clothes hanger shaped in the form of a question mark, he said, serves as a permanent and unavoidable reminder to check the lights, oven, windows, furnace, appliances, and doors whenever they leave the house, especially before leaving on a trip.

When he mentioned the specific items to check, I asked the class to create an acronym to hold each of these important items in mind. The best answer of all was the one that rearranged the order of items this way: *d*oors, *a*ppliances, *w*indows, *o*ven, *l*ights, and *f*urnace. DA WOLF!

The Floor Reminder

If you do not want a constant reminder hanging on your

doorknob, you can still remind yourself of things as you leave your house simply by placing that letter you have to mail, or the thing you have to take or deliver, on the floor right next to or in front of the door, where you cannot miss it.

Another of my seminar students sometimes gets his best ideas in the middle of the night or just before he dozes off. When this happens he no longer has to get up to write the thought down. He uses the floor reminder instead. He reaches for his pack of cigarettes (anything else will do), and he tosses it on the floor, scattering a few cigarettes. He makes a quick association between the cigarettes and the idea he wants to remember, and then he forgets about it and goes back to sleep. In the morning he can't miss those cigarettes on the floor. They instantly cue his idea, and he writes it down in detail over a cup of coffee.

Another "wee hours of the morning" reminder that works was used recently by my publisher. He told me that at about 3:00 one morning he thought of three important ideas but was too tired to get up and write them down. Suddenly, he remembered reading a sample chapter I had submitted for this book, which taught the Brain Chain technique. He decided to try it, and he linked those three ideas into a mental chain. Then he just went back to sleep. The next morning those three ideas came to him loud and clear via the Brain Chain, and he was able to put them into action.

This, of course, was an internal reminder. Actually, he could have created extra memory insurance by taking his alarm clock (or any other object within reach), making a mental association between it and the first item in his Brain Chain, and then just placing that clock or magazine on the carpet where he couldn't miss it in the morning. This would be his reminder to remember the Brain Chain upon awakening and to recall the links.

The principle behind the floor reminder and other external reminders is simply changing the immediate environment in such a way that it lightens your memory load by effectively reminding you to do what you have to do. There is no more dependable reminder, for instance, than hanging the suit that has to be cleaned on your front doorknob. How can you possibly forget this as you leave?

The Rubber Band Reminder

Another useful reminder is something I think of as the Lepkin reminder. A psychologist friend by that name showed it to me one night, and it works like a charm. Lepkin keeps a rubber band on his dashboard, and during trips when his car is approaching a tunnel, he takes the rubber band (after he turns on his headlights) and stretches it from a radio knob to his shifting gear. In this stretched position, he cannot help but keep noticing it. If he leaves it like this, it is a distraction, just like the telephone receiver in the reversed position. So, after he comes out of the other end of the tunnel, the stretched rubber band is his reminder to turn off his headlights. He then removes the band and hangs it back on the radio knob.

You can take this a step further and use the rubber band to remind you to release your emergency brakes, to fill the gas tank, or whatever other such remembering is necessary. You do not have to stretch the band from your radio knob to your shifting gear. Depending on your car's dashboard arrangement, you can stretch a rubber band in many ways and directions.

The Paper Clip Cue

Keep a small paper clip in your pocket or purse to "clip" things in your memory. Just make a quick mental picture between what has to be done and the paper clip and then clip it to your wristwatch band in a way that keeps the clip visible to you. Or you can attach the clip to the end of your sleeve or even clip it to your ring, if you like. In any of these places, you will be sure to notice the clip repeatedly, and it will be a constant reminder.

TACTILE REMINDERS

This category is for reminders that you actually feel, rather than those that are primarily seen or heard. For relief from the following tactile reminders, you must first do the thing they are reminding you to do. Because of this characteristic, this class of reminders is more compelling. These reminders are especially practical for people who put off doing things they know must be done. Read these ideas with an open mind and try one or two that appeal to you. It wouldn't surprise me if more than a few people feel that these reminders alone are worth the price of the book.

The Ring Reminder

This is an old idea, but if you have never actually tried it, its usefulness and effectiveness will surprise you. It works best if you do not wear more than one or two rings. When something occurs to you that you don't want to forget, just remove your ring from one hand and place it on the other hand. Use any finger you choose. The more peculiar it feels or looks to you the better.

The secret of making the ring reminder effective is simple. Do *not* put the ring back on the original finger until you have done what you were being reminded to do! I have used this device for years, and it has never failed me. You must, of course, make a mental picture association between what you want to remember and the ring itself; otherwise you can easily forget what it is that the ring is trying to tell you. For example, if you must remember an important meeting today, you could picture a small red piece of meat (*meet*ing) on the ring instead of a stone. If the meeting is with your boss or one person only, picture him or her sitting on your ring and waving to you. Whatever you visualize *vividly* will do the job.

If you cannot remove your ring in the first place, or if you prefer not to remove it, the ring reminder can still work. Just turn the ring around so that its stone or top design faces your palm. If your ring has something on it such as a stone or raised top, you will feel the difference in this position, and that is all you need to remind you.

A variation, if this is possible, is just to put your ring on a different finger on the same hand. You will feel it even more in this way. It will still feel and look out of place to you, and this is the whole idea.

Another variation that works well is simply to push your ring up to the first joint you come to (where your finger bends in the middle) and leave it there. In this way, every time you bend your finger you will feel that reminder.

One final variation is to remove your ring, put it into your pocket, and leave it there until you perform the required action. Then reward yourself by putting your ring back on. If noticing that your ring is missing bothers you, this "absent reminder" will do the trick.

The Wristwatch Reminder

Basically, this works like the ring reminder. Your wristwatch goes where you go, and therefore you can always use it. But this idea has an extra advantage to it, because you can tighten your wristwatch band a notch or two so that it will be a wee bit uncomfortable. Do not make it so tight, of course, that it irritates you. This would only defeat your purpose, because you will end up loosening it again before you do what it is supposed to remind you to do. But if it is just the slightest bit tight, it will be a stronger reminder if you so desire.

As with the ring reminder, a variation is to swing your watch around so that the face is on the same side as your palm. If this draws your attention to the watch, use it. If it doesn't, forget it. It must feel and/or look unusual in some way in order to get your periodic attention and thereby function as an effective reminder. In this way, sooner or later, you will perform the necessary duty if only to get rid of that nagging reminder.

Again, another effective variation is to remove your watch and put it on your *other* wrist until the job is done. For really important things to do, remember that you can still tighten the wrist band a bit to give the reminder extra power. Remember, the trick is not to relieve yourself by replacing the watch until you accomplish your intention.

Tie, Sleeve, Shoelace, and Belt Reminders (Industrial-Strength Reminders)

Within limits, tightening the watchband can be a very potent reminder. This idea can be extended to your tie, sleeve, shoelaces, and belt, because each of these things can be tightened as well. Within reason you can pull up your sleeve until it resists, tighten your shoelace, tighten your tie, and even tighten your belt a notch or two. Any of these reminder reinforcements will create an industrial-strength reminder, if and when needed. Such reminders will not *let* you forget.

Human nature being what it is, it is sometimes helpful if we can make ourselves remember certain things we have to do. It is only for times like these that you should use any of these more compelling reminders. Otherwise, under normal conditions, any of the other external reminders will do their jobs admirably.

The Pocket or Purse Displacement Reminder

If your keys, coins, comb, or wallet are each in a particular pocket, you can use this fact to your advantage as a tactile reminder. Just take an item that you always have in a certain pocket and place it in a different pocket. Make your mental picture as usual and then just let this displacement principle do your remembering for you. You will feel periodically aware of the strange lump or weight in the wrong pocket.

If your purse is compartmentalized and you keep things in an organized fashion, you can use the displacement idea to change the location of your powder, wallet, lipstick, or any other item you want to use as a reminder. Just looking in your purse will alert you to the fact that something is different, and as soon as you see the item in the wrong place you will be reminded of a specific intention.

TO PICTURE OR NOT TO PICTURE

Some external reminders require no mental picturing in order to work. These would include hanging a suit or dress on the doorknob, ready to be taken to the cleaners, or putting the monthly bills on your desk where you will see them. These and other such direct reminders require no mental picturing because when you come upon them you see the picture at a glance and know immediately what has to be done with these things themselves.

Other external reminders require a moment of mental picturing in order for them to do their job. However, there is another way that you can accomplish the same thing that mental picturing can do, and you may prefer it. It is sometimes quicker and easier. I refer to the simple talking technique you learned in Chapter 5, in which you mentally spoke to yourself or when you put an item in a place that you wished to remember so that you could retrieve it later on.

In other words, instead of always forming a mental picture with a ring, paperclip, or wristwatch, you can also talk to that external reminder itself and tell it what to remind you of. Make your instructions short and definite as in the Talking Technique of Chapter 5. Picturing and the Talking Technique both do the same thing; they force you to concentrate on and register what you intend to remember. In this sense you are still reinforcing an external reminder with an internal reminder.

Either the picturing or spoken reinforcement (or both) will work. As to which works better in certain situations, a little practice with each method will give you the answer.

EAR REMINDERS

In recent years, the alarm clock has acquired a new feature called the snooze alarm. This refinement is the clock's ability to beep or buzz repeatedly at certain intervals to keep reminding you to wake up. On my last birthday my children gave me one of these snooze alarms; it is programmed to emit four short beeps, with a one-second interval between each set of four beeps. Whenever I hear it I automatically hear, "Dad-dy-wake-up! Dad-dy-wake-up!" External reminders that repeat themselves have a special power to coax, cajole, and finally compel you to take action. The snooze alarm is something you *hear*. The rubber band, ring, and floor reminders, plus others, are external reminders that can be seen, felt, or heard, or all three together. The point is that, unlike internal reminders by themselves, many external reminders are *repeatable* in effect because they continue to remind you whenever you see, hear, or feel them. *This* is the reason that external reminders are so effective.

The Wristwatch Alarm Reminder

These handy little alarms have so many uses that only your own imagination can limit them. Many business and professional people find them such useful reminders for time control that they do not want to be without them. Basically, you just associate what you want to remember with the watch, not the sound of the alarm. You cannot picture sound. When the alarm goes off you look at your watch, and your mental picture connection will recall the thing to do.

The following are just a few possible uses for the wristwatch alarm reminder:

- Appointments: Set the alarm ahead to give you preparation time.
- A reminder that it is time to start something.
- A reminder that the time is up.
- A reminder to do a specific thing then and there.
- A reminder that something important is happening somewhere at that moment.
- A reminder that your speech or visit is too long.
- A timely reminder to resist the temptation to say or do something you promised yourself you would not do.

Many businesspeople let their wristwatch alarms get rid of

visitors who stay too long. They set their alarm for a certain time, just before the visitor enters. Later, when the alarm sounds, the executive says nothing, but merely looks at his watch as he shuts off the alarm. He keeps smiling, but the message gets across.

THE ARC METHOD: REMEMBERING ANYTHING YOU STUDY OR READ

The ARC Method is a surprisingly effective and virtually effortless method for learning and remembering almost anything you read, hear, or study. The method is so obvious that it is amazing that many people either do not know about it or haven't tried it. Back in school, the only way we knew of learning anything involved, difficult, or lengthy was to read it, study it, or recite it—over and over. Rote repetition was the order of the day, and to a large extent it still prevails. Of course common sense tells you that if you repeat anything over and over long enough, eventually you will have it memorized. However, everyone also knows that such rote learning is boring, time-consuming, tedious, and difficult to force ourselves to do. This kind of repetition easily becomes mindless, unthinking, parrotlike repetition, and because of this, whatever is so "memorized" can quickly become inaccessible to recall after a short period of time.

The technique I am about to teach you requires little if any effort on your part. It can be used anytime, anyplace, and it will accommodate almost any kind of material, regardless of length or difficulty. You do not have to do any repeating of any sort; as a matter of fact, you don't even have to pay close attention to the material while you are learning it, if you choose not to. All you need is a small piece of equipment: a cassette recorder, any kind of cassette recorder at all.

This is the method: Decide what it is that you want to learn and remember, or memorize, and then record that material on a cassette. If it is reading material, read it onto the cassette. If it is a joke or story or quotation, just tell the joke, read the quote or story, and record it. The next step is to let the playback do all the work for you.

For example, suppose you have four or five pages of material that you must know by next Tuesday morning. Read the text into your cassette recorder and then let the recorder do all the repeating that you feel is necessary. You just listen, rewind, listen, rewind, and keep this up for as long and as often as you feel necessary to become thoroughly familiar with the material.

What is important to remember with this method is that you do *not* have to sit and listen and concentrate. Of course it will not hurt if you do; but if you have a few days to listen to the material at odd moments during the day—when you are shaving, doing the dishes, eating, or driving your car—the material (besides being understood and enjoyed, as in contrast to rote) will inevitably work its way, without any help from you, directly into your mind and memory. If you can sit and give it your undivided attention, you will, of course, learn it faster. But this is not necessary. Merely hearing it at various times now and then, over and over, over a period of an hour, a day, or days, depending on the length of the material and your deadline, will do the trick for you.

A friend of mine recently told me she was preparing for her Master's Degree exam in English literature. She is a busy homemaker and mother, and she was worried about not having enough time to devote to studying. There was a lot of material she had to know. I suggested that she write down all the questions she thought might be asked on the exam and assemble complete answers to these questions. I then told her to record the materials on her cassette along with selected pages of text and then just play it back every day at various convenient times that she could not ordinarily use for study purposes. I told her to play the material regardless of what she was doing—cooking, washing dishes, doing the laundry. The little cassette recorder could always be placed nearby. All she had to do was rewind the tape periodically for another replay whenever she felt like pushing the playback button.

Not long after I gave her this idea she telephoned me to say that not only did this study method give her a tremendous amount of extra learning time, but it enabled her to learn all the material so well, so completely, and so easily that she passed her exam with flying colors. She also mentioned that her normal pre-exam jitters and anxiety were greatly reduced and that she felt extremely confident in her knowledge after all of that repetitive reinforcement of the material. She told me she only wished that she had known of this kind of effortless learning reinforcement years ago. She said it not only would have saved her great amounts of time, but that it would have been far easier and more productive. She was also certain that she would remember the material better and retain it longer than if she had studied or crammed with the usual, conventional methods.

I call this method the ARC Method: Automatic Repetition by Cassette. If you have use for such a method, be sure to try it. I think you will be surprised and impressed with the results. Many professional speakers learn their speeches this way. It saves time and makes the learning of key points, details, jokes, stories, anecdotes, and technical materials easier to absorb and remember.

Remember that you will get even better (and faster) results if you actively participate by concentrating your attention on what you hear and reciting the material periodically as you listen to the tape. Remember that recitation is rehearsing actual retrieval of the material. That is why recitation is so effective as a learning process. If you want to make this cassette reinforcement idea work even better, combine it with relaxed recitation every now and then during your playback periods.

You probably will not find this method recommended in formal study books; but neither were hundreds of other such valuable ideas accepted or recommended for years—until all of a sudden they were "discovered" or somehow rediscovered, becoming not only acceptable but of great benefit to great numbers of people as well.

So there you have it. For those who are interested, there are some specially made cassette tapes which automatically play and repeat themselves continuously, for the purpose of constant, uninterrupted repetition. What they do, basically, is save you the time of rewinding your cassette each time you come to the end of the tape.

I am very interested in the results you attain with this ARC method. If you care to let me know how it works for you, and/or what new ideas you have used successfully with it, please write me in care of the publisher.

PHOTOGRAPHIC MEMORY: THE INSTANT CAMERA FOR NAMES, FACES, AND FACTS ABOUT PEOPLE

If you have a camera that makes instant pictures, here is a quick, convenient, and ingenious way of successfully prolonging your memory for people's names and faces and for facts about people. It can enable you to see them months or years later and not only remember their names and faces, but also where they work, their spouses' names, children's names, and any other useful facts originally learned about them. This is powerful stuff, and if it is worth the comparatively small amount of time and effort you invested for such results, you will be very glad to know about this system.

The method consists of a combination of the CCR names and faces method and the use of an instant camera. As with the previous combination of internal and external reminder methods (mental filing and later recording this information on cassette), you first remember people with the CCR (or SALT) System; then you get their pictures permanently with your instant camera.

Clearly, you must use this idea only for certain people you really want to remember. You can hardly shoot pictures of everyone you meet unless you are a millionaire camera bug. In addition, you have to think of an acceptable reason for taking a quick shot of an individual or a group. With a little imagination you can come up with something plausible. Saying it's for the company or club archives is frequently sufficient, even if you are not the official photographer.

Another idea is for you to invent a reason for wanting to have *your* picture taken with them. They may be even more flattered and willing to cooperate. Many times people do not even ask why you want their picture. They just agree out of courtesy. Also remember that you can always promise an extra instant snapshot for *them* to keep, as an inducement if necessary. Many people cannot resist having another photograph of themselves, especially a free one.

After you shoot your pictures, take pen in hand at your earliest opportunity, that same day or evening, and write the correct names directly under the appropriate person or persons on the bottom of the print. A fine-point permanent marker pen is best for this. For *facts* about persons, use the back of the print. *This* is the time to write in *all* the information you want to remember about these people.

It is also a good idea to write in the original name and face connections you made when meeting these people. In this way you can easily relearn them at a later date and still actually recognize and call the individuals by name when you see them again.

Whenever you expect to see this important person or persons again, all you have to do is whip the print out of your file. If you have forgotten the name, face, or any of the facts you knew about them, you can easily rememorize them now with your original CCR connections or, if you prefer, with entirely new associations. If you are about to meet just one or two of these people again, chances are that after looking at the snapshots you will *know* their names without even applying the CCR System to relearn them.

Take as much time as you like with this review. There's no hurry. The prints won't fade, and you can look forward to impressing the people you are about to see again, as you confidently call them by name, ask about their spouses and kids by name, and use some of the other pertinent facts as well.

Remember, after this procedure, you really *do* remember these people's names, and you are now ready to meet and greet them properly, as they have never been remembered before! They will probably never forget you.

Although you may not know of this instant camera method of ensuring future memory for names, it has been used for years by clever people who realize that the effort involved is far exceeded by the benefits.

A variation of this technique was illustrated in a recent movie with Alan Alda. Alda played the part of an up-and-coming young U.S. senator named Joe Tynan. In one scene he tells a subordinate to place a long-distance call to an important contact. As the connection is made the senator tries to think of the man's first name, and instantly his assistant pulls the proper file card from a voluminous name-index file situated close by. Without skipping a beat Senator Tynan (now viewing the file card), is able to greet his contact with, "Hello, Henry!" Later, before ending the conversation (with the card still in view), the senator also "remembers" Henry's *wife's* name, and sends her his personal regards as well!

Please have no doubts that such records are kept and *used*, not only by politicians, but by intelligent, clever, and ambitious people in many other fields as well. Senator Tynan's system works only for telephone conversations; but with the CCR System, plus an instant camera and a notated print file, you can use the technique not only over the telephone, but for face-to-face meetings as well.

STANDARD REMINDERS

The Written Reminder

By far, the most frequently used external memory aid is writing things down. Most of the world's achievers have been habitual note takers. They kept voluminous notes and files and eventually these materials found their way into print. As a result of this, books and libraries have become the "memory of man."

Making written notations about important things to remember sounds like the obvious thing to do, but the number of people who do not do this is still surprisingly large. Either they do not want to be bothered or they think they can keep everything in their heads. As a result of not taking notes or using other memory aids, the efficiency and productiveness of such people is usually far below those of people who do use such reminder methods.

As I have said many times before, do not hesitate to write things down. The advent of writing materials changed the course of the world. But remember that when circumstances make writing things down inconvenient or impossible, you now have eminently workable and efficient Memory Control techniques to keep these facts, names, and ideas in mind for you *until* you can get them down on paper later on.

When you do make notations, do not fall into the trap of using different scraps of paper for each reminder, unless you feel this system works well for you. The problem is that all of your scraps of paper are too easy to misplace, lose, or forget to consult. It does not matter whether your personal note pad is simple or fancy as long as it is easy to write on and easy to find. It must be accessible to be of any use.

If you have a secretary, use him or her as a valuable external reminder and have your notations periodically typed into a neat list for your desk, pocket, or purse.

Many busy people use several written reminder systems: a pocket note pad for instant use anytime, a desk calendar for appointments and things to do, and a desk book for more extensive notations. I do not recommend that you become a slave to your notations, but the use of such commonsense external memory aids is easier and more effective than trying to remember all the details of day-to-day business, social, and family life.

Reminders That Stare You in the Face

When you want to be reminded of the current status of any changing situation, many kinds of visual aids (external reminders) can do such remembering for you. To name just a few, there are color-coded wall charts, magnet-label charts, wall graphs, erasable-marker writing surfaces, wall-mounted boards with pockets for instant switching of cards to show current position or sales volume, and so on.

If wall space is at a minimum, you can get self-adhesive cork bulletin board squares to fit available space. By putting such reminders where you *must* see them, you are changing your environment and making it do some important remembering for you.

A REVIEW OF EXTERNAL REMINDERS

People need reminders. Reminders trigger your memory's performance. To a very large extent all you really need are effective reminders in order to remember *anything* successfully. With external reminders, the trick is simply to make a noticeable change in your surroundings and let it jog your memory.

An external reminder must be easy to see, hear, or feel so that it will instantly retrieve the desired information. All the reminders in this chapter fit the "see, hear, or feel" categories. In some cases they combine two or all three of these characteristics.

For easy reference, all preceding external reminders will now be classified into these three categories.

Reminders You See

1. The Telephone Reminder
2. The Answering Machine Reminder
3. The Doorknob Reminder
4. The Floor Reminder

5. The Rubber Band Reminder
6. The Paper Clip Cue
7. The Instant Camera Reminder
8. The Written Reminder
9. Reminders That Stare You in the Face

Reminders You Hear

10. The Wristwatch Alarm
11. Tape Recorder

Reminders You Feel

12. The Ring Reminder
13. The Wristwatch Reminder
14. Industrial-Strength Reminders
15. Pocket or Purse Displacement Technique

CRITERIA FOR EXTERNAL REMINDERS

I have isolated four characteristics that determine the effectiveness of external reminders. When one or more of these is present, the power of the reminder is increased.

1. The reminder should be active: By this I mean it should do something to attract your attention. If it can be seen, heard, felt, or sensed strongly in some way, it is an *active* reminder.

2. The reminder should be specific: After the reminder initially attracts your attention, it should instantly trigger associations that represent and convey something specific. For example, it may remind you to mail a letter, make a bank deposit, keep an appointment, or any other *specific* thing or action.

3. The reminder should be repeatable: The snooze alarm is a good example of a repeatable reminder. If it does not get you to wake up the first time, it will do so sooner or later, because it keeps repeating itself. For certain types of remembering this feature is obviously desirable. It is interesting to note that many external reminders have this feature to one extent or another. If it is a "see" reminder, you cannot help but notice it over and over again. If it is a "feel" reminder, you continue to feel it periodically until you replace the ring on the right finger, put your wristwatch back on your other wrist, return an item to its correct pocket, or loosen your tie.

4. The reminder should be timely: A reminder that can prompt you at the right time is all the more useful. Not all external reminders can do this. Some that can do this are the snooze alarm, the wristwatch alarm, the doorknob and floor reminders, and the telephone reminder.

REMEMBERING TO REMEMBER

External reminders can also be used to remind you to review your mentally filed information. When you file a list of things to do or to think about, no benefits will accrue if you forget to do this. Remember that *anything* you have previously committed to memory and that needs reviewing can instantly be brought to mind with the use of an appropriate external cue.

For memory tasks and problems in the "things to do" category, remember that one of the quickest ways to improve your memory's performance is not to use your own memory at all, but, whenever possible, to have the things in your environment do the remembering *for* you. Next time you have to remember something to do, ask yourself, not "How will I remember this?" but instead, "Where can I put something that will remind me of this?"

These external retrieval cues are genuinely effective memory joggers. Now that you know about them, remember to let them save you time, effort, and the frustration of forgetting. Just use the ones that appeal to you and that fit your needs. Used properly, they will not let you down.

12

The Retrieval of
Lost Memories

You now know how to put information into your mind in such a way that you can get it back out again when you need it. But what about those things in your experience *prior* to reading this book? What about the things that occurred minutes, hours, weeks, months, or years ago, which you have forgotten but may want to remember?

Let's take first things first. Your memory is your only connection with the past; the key word here is *connection*. If you can find that connection, you can retrieve the memory in the great majority of cases. The problem and the solution are to find the right connections.

When you commit something to memory with one of our memory techniques, there is an immediacy of control that does not exist with past information you learned or experienced *without* the application of such a control strategy. In other words, you have no immediate and direct access to such past learning unless you *do* remember it. without any trouble. But if that name or fact or idea is forgotten, the only way to bring it back is to find an original connection or retrieval cue to bring it back *for* you. For the rest of this chapter, we will explore ways and means of finding and discovering those hidden cues.

Again, it is important to realize that whenever you say you "can't remember" something (no matter how long ago it happened), what you are really saying is that you can't find the right retrieval cue to pull that name or fact out of your subconscious and into your conscious mind. Remember, it is still there, but it is resisting retrieval because nothing is accessible at the moment to retrieve it! It is available, but not accessible.

THE MENTAL PROBE

This situation is the same as when a secretary knows that a needed document is in the files somewhere but cannot remember where it is. In a situation like this, it is not very effective to keep rummaging through a file drawer where the file folder ought to be but isn't. After carefully searching that drawer without results, the intelligent secretary starts thinking of other possible headings or subheadings under which the missing information might have been filed. Realizing the quirks of the human mind, the secretary would let his or her imagination begin to seek out some of the unlikely but possible places for further search.

Your mind is a vast filing system. When you start to search your own mind for a lost idea or fact you must be as flexible and imaginative as that secretary searching for a misplaced file. If you keep looking in one place over and over, you accomplish nothing except to increase your frustration and waste time. Instead, probe your mind repeatedly for the right retrieval cue, just as the secretary tries to think of other headings under which the missing material might be hiding. The secret is to look in other places.

Think back to the time when you first learned the information or the last time you used it. Let your imagination go to work for you. What other kind of associative connections might have been used for such information? Continue probing your mind with "how?" "where?" "when?" "why?" "who?" and so on. Under what other novel, offbeat, or special heading could you have filed it? The trick is to keep up such a procedure until you discover the probe that hits the target. Many times this approach will work for you very quickly. Other times it may take longer, and sometimes it won't seem to work at all during your first session of such probing and searching. If this happens, leave it alone for a while and try again later. The point is that, if the information is really important to you, you shouldn't give up too easily. It's there, all right; you just have to find it. You have the world's greatest filing system between your ears; it is up to you to become a good file clerk.

Sometimes the answer will just pop into your mind when you least expect it, minutes, hours, or days later. Many forgotten memories are instantly brought to life by a chance encounter with the right retrieval cue. If all attempts fail, however, and you still need the information, the following method may work for you.

WORKING WITH YOUR SUBCONSCIOUS MIND

With this technique you talk directly to your subconscious mind and command it to deliver. For years I read about this technique, usually in books on self-hypnosis. Although I did not necessarily hypnotize myself, I did deliberately try to relax, usually at night before going to sleep. As calmly and confidently as I could, I would then speak to my subconscious mind, telling it that it was to deliver to me tomorrow morning at 8:00 A.M. whatever information I needed.. I must admit that the first couple of times I tried this approach it did not work. But the third time it did indeed work, and I was surprised, delighted, and *impressed*.

I use such self-suggestion today, whenever necessary, and though it does not work every time, it works often enough for me to consider it a practical and valuable method. Sometimes I use this method not so much for material I can't remember, but for information I need to make a decision. For example, I pondered for days over the best way to organize various materials for this book. Finally, I decided to forget it for a while and let my subconscious solve the problem for me.

Before falling asleep one night, I closed my eyes and instructed my subconscious mind to give me the best possible answer to my problem the next morning shortly after I would wake up. It worked, but I almost lost it because I tried too hard the next morning to "hear" what, if anything, my subconscious was about to tell me. Nothing happened. After a while I got some orange juice, and then I started to shave. It wasn't long before I suddenly "saw" the correct succession of those troublesome chapter subjects in my mind's eye. The arrangement I perceived was obviously *so* right and sensible that I couldn't imagine why I had not thought of it before.

As you can see, I have no doubt that this method works for me. It must work for many other people, because I have read about it for many years in many books, and not all of them on hypnosis. So I urge you to try this approach and to give it a good and fair try when you use it. Give it a few chances to work for you before deciding anything. It is quite possible that it will work much faster for you than it did for me, especially if you can prime yourself to expect it to happen.

I will tell you in detail exactly how to speak to your subconscious mind when you use this method. First, wait until you are in bed and drowsy. Relax, close your eyes, and then say to your subconscious, clearly and confidently (but mentally) something like this: "The information I need is as follows. Mention the information you need. Then: "Therefore you are to give me this information tomorrow at 8:00 A.M. so that I can use this information properly." Repeat the instruction once more, and end by saying, "At 8:00 A.M. you will give me this information." Then forget it and go to sleep.

Experience has taught me that when I address my subconscious as "you," as though I am speaking to a person, it works better for me. Remember that repeating your instructions once or twice, always with calm authority, has a definite, positive effect. After you achieve success with this approach, you don't have to wait for bedtime. If you learn how to relax completely during the day, you can use the same method to give you faster answers, perhaps that same day, a few hours later. I must admit that I have never tried this, but judging from the voluminous literature on this method and its variations, including this "same day service" request, I see no reason for it not to work this way as well.

Elsewhere in this book I mentioned that my philosophy in memory education is to use, teach, and recommend any kind of memory technique or aid that works, whether it is an internal or external reminder or any other kind that does the job for you. With this in mind I offer you this Self-Suggestion Technique as an addition to your growing repertoire of memory strategies.

THE RECONSTRUCTION TECHNIQUE

As an example of how effectively you can search your mind, and by doing so, reconstruct past events in detail, I offer the following illustration. This method is something we all begin to use occasionally to bring to mind a past experience or event; but we usually do not really persevere, and as a result we come up with no or far too little information. The following actual occurrence will give you some idea of what we are all capable of with a little sustained effort.

As an exercise, I asked one of my seminar students if she could recall what she was doing on the evening of February 13, which was approximately ten months earlier. I told her to take whatever time she needed in order to come up with the answer, and to try hard. The following is a transcription of her reaction.

"Of course not! That was months and months ago. You're really not serious, are you? *Are* you? You are. Well, I don't see how anyone could get to first base with a question like that. I'm telling you now that I have no idea what I did that night, but if you really want me to try, I suppose I can do that much. Let's see—last February 13—that's almost a year ago!

February 13. Well, one thing I know, it was the day before Valentine's Day, February 14th. Let's see—Valentine's Day. Rob always takes me out to dinner on Valentine's Day. We were probably thinking about it. One of us always phones for a reservation a day or two before. The only thing I remember vaguely is the problem I had trying to find the right Valentine card when I was shopping.

Wait a minute. The card I bought wasn't right, and I took it back. I spent a lot of time shopping. That's all I can think of, shopping. The card I finally gave Rob must've been a good one because I think he said that this time he'd have to take me to a special place instead of our usual candlelight supper at Dominick's.

Wait! It *was* special. We went to a new restaurant on the North Side. It was, uh, Julian's. I remember because I called for the reservation, and the man said that they would call *us* the day before we came, to confirm the reservation. Otherwise they wouldn't hold it. He did call, because I remember when my little boy called me in from the backyard, he said that a "Julian man wanted me to eat dinner." This had to be the night you asked about because Julian *did* call the day before we went there. I remember Rob laughing at what our little boy said when we were having dinner in the kitchen. We had dinner at home, so that has to be what I was doing on that night of February 13."

What was first thought to be impossible to remember, was, in this way, successfully reconstructed, bit by bit. Through pure association, this woman gradually recalled a chain of events. One thing simply led to another, and a past event was sufficiently recreated.

This "reconstruct and remember" concept is used in various therapies, notably psychoanalysis. It is now also used in investigative procedures; it has proven valuable in helping witnesses remember past events with more accuracy. There is no reason why you cannot or should not use the power of this reconstruction technique when needed. This approach, plus a little patience, may surprise you.

Remembering a Forgotten Name

Let's say that you just can't seem to remember a particular name, and you have a few moments to think about it. Begin reconstructing as follows: Take a piece of paper and make a circle about an inch in diameter in the middle. Next, jot down all the things you *do* remember about that particular person anywhere except in the circle. Where did you meet? When? What color was his or her hair? What time was it? Why were you together? What did you talk about? What kind of voice did he or she have? high, low, medium? Is he or she married or single? What kind of work does the person do? What are the individual's hobbies?

Just keep writing all the things that come to mind about the person, and at some point during this process all those things will link up. Then, suddenly—click!—up comes that name. Now write the name in the circle, and you have it. About 80 to 90 percent of the time, if you use this technique when you experience a memory block for a name, this will work. On paper, you surround the circle of forgotten information with retrieval cues until something clicks.

It is *not* a good idea to try to concentrate on something you just can't remember. If the name is gone, don't try to force it back through wasted concentration, because you will literally be concentrating on nothing.

HANDLING MOMENTARY MENTAL BLANKS— THE STARTING OVER METHOD

Everyone occasionally experiences a momentary mental blank. You are human; this is to be expected, and it is really nothing to worry about. For example, let's say you are reading a newspaper or magazine and you suddenly feel hungry and want a quick snack. You go into the kitchen, and you find yourself thinking, "What am I doing in here?" If you stand there racking your brain, you probably won't remember. But if you go *back* into the living room, sit down and start to read again, in a moment or so this very act will do the trick. All of a sudden you'll think, "Oh! A slice of that turkey and a Coke!"

There are two reasons for this sudden rush of recall:

1. You returned to exactly what you were doing and *where* you were doing it when the original impulse sent you to the kitchen.
2. You let your mind relax again. This gave your mind easier access to what it wanted to remember.

By starting over, your mind is able to catch the thread of association again and prompt you once more with the original thought. Psychologists call this phenomenon *state-dependent recall*. When you recreate the state you were in originally, the memory returns.

It is always a good idea not to let yourself become impatient, upset, or frustrated just because you have momentarily forgotten something. Instead, say to yourself, "It is not accessible to me at the moment. It will come back soon." Then leave it alone! Let your subconscious go to work for you and come up with the missing information.

RECAPTURING THE THREAD OF CONVERSATION:

"Now, What Were We Talking About?"

Every once in a while a person seems to lose the thread of conversation. Whatever the cause—inattention, a wandering mind, or some distraction—you suddenly realize that you have lost the point and you don't know what the conversation is about at all.

The cure for such a situation is just common sense, but many times, people get nervous when this happens and forget to use their heads. When you find that you have lost the thread of the conversation, the first thing to do is to listen hard to the other speaker or speakers and see if you can pick up a retrieval cue or two to trigger the conversation topic for you. The trick, of course, is simply to be a very good listener until you catch the missing thread. Of course, if you were a good listener in the first place, this probably wouldn't have happened. But you are human, not a robot, and these things occur. If it does happen, don't allow yourself to become uneasy. Stay relaxed, close your mouth, open your ears, and listen for a good retrieval cue. Do not be afraid of a little silence in the conversation. Sometimes a bit of silence helps your mind remember the missing point, without having to keep listening at the same time.

If all your efforts to recapture the conversational thread seem futile, there comes a time when honesty is the best policy. Just smile and mention that you seem to have lost the point and let someone put you back into the picture.

"Now, What Was I Talking About?"

Occasionally your mind may go out to lunch while *you* are talking. The basic problem is the same, but the solution is different. This time you cannot simply close your mouth, open your ears, and wait. This is a quirk that has bedeviled public speakers since time immemorial. I will give you two simple ideas that work either on the platform or in social conversation. Use your own judgment in applying them.

The Whatever Method

As soon as you realize that your thoughts have deserted you, just think of whatever it was that you just finished saying and take that particular word, phrase, or idea, and continue to talk about it. For example, if you were speaking about the high crime rate, and the last word you remember yourself saying was *rate*, take that word, rate, and let it lead you. Talk about, and call attention to, the word *rate* itself and how ratings can apply to many things. Talk about the rate of speed, or progress, or decay, or interest—or *whatever* occurs to you at the moment. If you can continue in this way, something will eventually call your lost point back to your mind. Admittedly, this method may be better for the platform than it is for conversation. But if you can be creative, it can help.

The Pause Method

Speakers often pause to take a drink of water. What the audience does *not* know is that the speaker may be trying to remember what he was just talking about! A variation of this in social conversation is to search for your handkerchief, cigarettes, or pencil or to look thoughtfully at your watch for a moment or two. This is a variation of the Whatever Technique, because you are using whatever kind of delaying tactic you can think of to give you a moment or two to recover your lost thought. A practical reason for this little ploy, of course, is that if you remain preoccupied in silence long enough, someone else will quite naturally pick up where you left off, and *they* will do the talking. Chances are that their own words will bring back to your mind whatever it was that you had forgotten. In any event, it may be totally unnecessary for you now to even try to recall what you forgot, because the conversation is off and running again on its own.

The Unexpected Compliment

There is one other strategy that works as a cover-up rather than as an opportunity for you to recapture a forgotten thought while you are talking to others. I have seen this clever tactic in action more than once, and it always amuses me.

The next time you are speaking during a conversation and your memory goes to sleep, use that very moment to stop talking, look appreciatively at someone, and say, "Excuse me, Carol, but I can't help noticing that beautiful necklace you're wearing. Where did you find it?" She will not only pick up the conversation from that moment on, but she will love you for it. If you pick a man, you can suddenly appreciate his tie, shirt, suit, tan, or whatever.

Whoever you select for this unexpected compliment will surely answer delightedly, thus continuing the conversation. The fact that you forgot what you were saying will now be unnoticed and irrelevant. The point is that it may not always be necessary for you to worry about remembering what you forgot, if you use a little imagination.

Part III:
Fine Points

When I was younger I could remember
anything whether it happened or not.
Mark Twain

13

How to Know
Which Methods to Use
and When

Now that I finally got it all together, I forgot where I put it!

Anonymous

We have covered a lot of material, and now it is time to try to bring it all into focus. First, since every fact or idea is potentially forgettable, there are three things you can do for the things you really want to remember:

1. Deliberately decide what is important enough to commit to memory. Many things can be safely stored in writing or looked up in books. On the other hand, many names, numbers, facts, ideas, or other information may be needed frequently and at a moment's notice. These are the things you should consider committing to memory. It is up to you to decide which is which.

2. Decide on the particular Memory Control technique that is most appropriate for the job. This, or creating your own memory aids based on principles learned, is an important part of Memory Control. Not only is this creative and fun, but your own original mnemonic ideas will work *better* for you.

3. Once you decide on the proper technique, use it.

Virtually all memory tasks and problems fall into one of two categories: *things to do* (intention or "action" memory); *things to know* (information or knowledge memory). For example, if you want to remember to attend a meeting at 3:00 P.M. today, or if you don't want to forget to have your brakes relined, or if you *do* forget to take care of a financial transaction, or if you forget to keep a promise to be home in time for dinner tonight, all such *intended* actions, whether remembered or forgotten, fall into the category of things to do.

On the other hand, if you want to remember someone's name, address, or phone number, or the name of a certain book, or the exact spot you left your wallet, or, if the answer to an exam question suddenly slips your mind, or if you're about to give a speech and your mind goes blank, or if you feel you may not remember the needed credit information now that you're at the bank, all of these situations in which you either remember or forget, fall into the memory category of things to know.

Now that these two main memory categories are isolated, it will be easier for you to choose the appropriate memory techniques that work best *within* one or the other of these memory divisions.

The first thing to do when a memory problem confronts you is to decide whether it belongs to the things to do or things to know department. Next, you select a control technique that handles that type of task and use it. Actually, some of the methods you have learned overlap and can be used in *either* of the two memory categories. After you have a little more practical experience with these techniques, you will know which ones work best for you.

For now we can list the two categories and the techniques for each, which work well for most people. Instead of things to do or things to know, you may prefer to think of these two categories as intentions and information, or simply action and knowledge.

THINGS TO DO
(INTENTION OR ACTION MEMORY)

This category usually concerns the things to be done that particular day. Any of the Mental Filing Systems will handle this nicely, especially if there is a *list* of such things to be done. If any of the things to get done apply to future days, it is best to let your dated tickler file or desk calendar pad remember this for you.

If only one or two things are to be remembered for action during the day, or if these are all you can think of at the moment, let your surroundings help you remember by using one of the external reminder techniques.

If you need to remember things in a particular sequence, any of the mental filing methods will work, including the Brain Chain. For remembering in numerical sequence, use the number-rhyme file system.

If you need to be reminded to review your mental files, or if you need to be reminded to remember something specific, use one of the appropriate external reminders to prompt you. If remembering to do something is particularly important or of an urgent nature, and you need a more compelling reminder, remember that any of the tightener external reminders discussed earlier will not *let* you forget!

THINGS TO KNOW
(INFORMATION OR KNOWLEDGE MEMORY)

Facts, ideas, reading material, and any other types of information belong in this memory category. Remember that the most natural memory aid for learning and retaining information is the word AID itself. It stands for *A*ttention, *I*nterest, and *D*esire. If you are *attentive* and have enough *interest* in and *desire* to learn and remember something, this alone can impress it on your memory. Such AID *plus* the appropriate memory technique is an unbeatable combination for reliable retention and recall.

Specific techniques for remembering where you put things, remembering numbers, and remembering names and faces are covered in separate chapters devoted to these subjects. Methods for mental recording of confidential information; speaking without notes; remembering what you read or hear; remembering facts about people; learning English or foreign vocabulary words; recalling calendar information; remembering birthdays, appointments, and events; and remembering jokes and special facts are covered in Chapter 10. Committing single or isolated facts to memory is covered in chapters 6, 9, and 10. Creative ideas for remembering such facts are shown in various mnemonic devices at the end of chapters 6 and 10.

The use of the tape recorder as a memory aid, plus the use of an instant camera for recalling names, faces, facts about people, plus material on written reminders, appears in Chapter 11. Certain other specifics and fine points not listed in this section can only be reviewed and remembered by rereading the appropriate chapters.

14

How to Keep Your New Memory Skills Sharp

Unlike other worthwhile skills that require weeks or months of practice before you begin to notice results, you know from your participation in our exercises that most Memory Control techniques work immediately. However, the real accomplishment and pleasure they can provide comes only with continuing practice and use.

THE *TRU-FLO* SECRETS OF MEMORY

Remember the TRU Formula for memory retention reinforcement. By occasionally thinking of the material, reviewing the idea or fact, and, above all, using the information, you can retain and recall information for as long as you desire.

Similarly, remember the natural FLO of your memory. Let this FLO Formula remind you of the great secret of memory: You can make *anything* easier to remember if you use it frequently, link things together mentally, and make things outstanding. By doing so, you intensify the substance and core of memory itself, meaning.

Good remembering is a skill that responds faithfully to training; but like other skills, if you don't use it, you can lose it. You

226

do not have to spend hours every day or week to develop your memory skills as you must with many other skills. The best way to practice and develop your expertise with Memory Control is just to *use* the techniques you have learned at every opportunity. Whenever you put something away that you want to locate later, take a moment or two to use the Talking Technique, or the multiple associations technique for long-term recall. Whenever the occasion arises to remember a new phone number, address, or date, use the Number-Meaning Method. Whenever you meet new people, use the SALT or CCR method, or both. The same applies to all other techniques you have learned.

For remembering larger chunks of information, including written material, the ARC Method (Automatic Repetition by Cassette) deserves your attention. This method provides you with extra time because you can learn by listening during normally unproductive hours while you drive, do housework, shave, or do anything else.

For names and faces an effective way to practice the CCR Method is to use it while you are seated in a restaurant, bus station, or any other place where many people are visible at close range. Mentally assign them names, one at a time, as you apply the method. After you have mentally met as many people as you like, you can recall the names you assigned them.

With a little practice, all the methods will work so well that you will look for opportunities to use them and polish them. Frankly, they are such fun to use, and so easy and effective, that they are an absolute delight. After a while, it may dawn on you, as it did on me years ago, what a priceless asset these methods are to know and use.

Here is one more way—a very good way—for you to keep your new memory control skills sharp. Simply teach them to others. In the very act of teaching your children, spouse, friends, or associates, you will be pleasantly forced to clarify, specify, explain, and demonstrate these techniques. Such teaching will not only benefit others, but it will give *you* greater personal conviction regarding the worth and lifelong value of these Memory Control skills.

As an external reminder, put this book somewhere you will be sure to notice it. Let it remind you to use what you have learned. By using your power to control your own memory, you will gain a new appreciation for and confidence in your memory's bursting potential and your new power to release and control it.

15

Final Thoughts: Mind Over Memory

What you have accomplished with the aid of this book provides a clear and convincing example of your ability to control your conscious mind, your working memory. In the last analysis, the techniques of Memory Control are literally a matter of mind over memory.

It seems appropriate in this last chapter to try to answer some questions about memory that are frequently asked by many of my seminar students.

Q: To what extent do a good memory and intelligence go together?

A: A person who effectively learns, retains, and remembers is demonstrating intelligence. A ready and efficient mind is admired by everyone, and we rarely forget the person with a good memory. With such things in mind, it is reasonable to assume that, for all practical purposes, a good memory and intelligence go hand in hand.

Dr. Gordon H. Bower of Stanford University, a leading expert in the psychology of memory, believes that a major difference between smart students and dull students lies in their use or non-use of learning strategies. The smart student knows how to remember, while the dull student does not. A study cited by Bower shows clearly that the significant differences in learning between normal and retarded children were practically eliminated when both of these groups used simple mnemonic techniques, especially mental imagery.*

Bower also cites typical experiments with college students in which the use of a loci mnemonic (similar to the house file system in Chapter 9) produced memory recall 700 percent greater than for those students not using a memory technique for the same material.**

This leads to the intriguing insight that "smart" people may simply be those who have discovered for themselves the power of mnemonic learning strategies and that they realize the immense value of such an asset in their lives. Since studies now show conclusively that the use of memory techniques makes fuller and more efficient use of the brain's own natural functioning, it seems obvious that, by *not* using such memory techniques, a person is effectively hindering his or her power to learn and remember!

With or without help from you, your brain continues to make its own associative, meaningful connections; but with a mnemonic *boost*, you can supercharge your memory cells far beyond their usual performance (not only as verified by Dr. Bower's report, showing a 700-percent improvement, but hopefully, with the results *you* have attained so far with the exercises in this book).

Methods to improve memory performance have been known for over twenty-five hundred years. Some of history's eminent names, figures who were among the pioneers in the classical memory methods, include the Greek poet Simonides; the Roman orator Cicero; the scholastic philosopher St. Thomas Aquinas; the scholar and humanist Petrarch; the philosopher Giordano

---

*Gordon H. Bower, "Analysis of a Mnemonic Device," *The American Scientist* 58 (1970), 496–510.
**Ibid.

Bruno; the mathematician Leibnitz; and the statesman and essayist Sir Francis Bacon, to name a few. As you can see, the art of memory has indeed kept good company.

Q: Since modern memory training is now available, why is it not taught more extensively in our schools and colleges?

A: Old ideas persist, and the results of the first experimental memory studies by Ebbinghaus as far back as 1885 still dominate today's educational picture. Ebbinghaus's findings emphasized learning primarily by repetition and influenced psychologists and educators away from the value of classical, applied mnemonics. This academic bias still exists.

Despite the fact that current modern research has long since acknowledged the power and value of mnemonic techniques, many educators have not freed themselves of these old biases. Also, many educators have not rid themselves of their image of mnemonics as "mental trickery" of doubtful practical value. This image is kept alive by the exploitation and exaggerated promotional claims of various insubstantial memory improvement books and courses, plus the performances of some memory experts whose theatrics and memory feats do not portray the art of memory as a practical, legitimate, and worthwhile study. As entertainment, such memory performances may be perfectly acceptable; but most educators remember this "showbiz" aspect of mnemonics, rather than the value of mnemonics as an educational tool of useful power and potential.

The phrase *artificial memory* is still used by educators in their references to memory systems. The thought of memory techniques as being in some way unnatural is ridiculous. The very things we have been working with throughout this book— association, meaning, visualization, etc.—*are the very things that the human mind works with most naturally and performs easiest and best.* Memory techniques do not replace these natural processes; instead, they use them and enhance their effectiveness through deliberate, conscious application. Anyone who considers such memory aids or techniques artificial or unnatural could hardly be more mistaken. It would be difficult indeed to find a more natural way to remember better than by using nature's own methods.

In spite of the obvious, old ideas die hard, and the world goes on as usual. The result is that students still depend on archaic methods of rote repetition and cramming. With few exceptions, our schools and colleges are still teaching what to know, but not how to remember it.

Q: What about memory and increasing age? Isn't it true that "the older you get, the more you forget?"

A: I feel that this is another harmful old saw. The problems of aging are many, but this does *not* necessarily include memory, in and of itself. You have only to read *The End of Senility* by Dr. Arthur A. Freese,* or any other modern and authoritative study on memory and aging, to become convinced, as I am, of the fallacy of inevitable memory deterioration with age.

The next time you come across an eighty-five or ninety-year-old who is obviously functioning mentally as well as you are (or better), ask what his or her secret is. Your answer will probably be a chuckle and the response that age is simply an attitude, and that you really shouldn't believe everything you hear about memory failure and age.

According to current findings, learning and memory do not begin to "decline" at any particular age at all. It has been known for years, for example, that a person's IQ score can go up at any age, especially after accumulated skills and experience develop with age. Learning simply builds on learning; the older you become, the more associations and experience you accumulate. The truth of the matter is simply that the more you learn, the more you *can* learn. Barring brain damage or psychological problems, aging itself sets the stage for better learning and remembering.

One of the reasons I enjoy the study and use of Memory Control techniques is because they are the kind of art and skill that can be used during my own later years to help keep me

*Dr. Arthur S. Freese, *The End of Senility* (New York: Arbor House, 1978), p. 43.

mentally fit and busy. I feel, as do many others, that continued and deliberate use of the mind, memory, and imagination may even contribute to longevity itself. Look at Bertrand Russell, George Santayana, or John Dewey. They, and others, were still going strong right up to their nineties.

The best example of this that I knew personally was David Roth, the famous memory expert of the early 1900s. I met him in 1968 at the first conference of the California Memory Research Center. At that time Dave was ninety-five. We became friends, and we corresponded for many months until his death at the age of ninety-seven. His last memory feat was to memorize a complete schedule of air travel distances between hundreds of cities all over the United States. He pioneered in the study of memory training, and he inspired and taught thousands of people from all walks of life that they could remember far better than they had ever thought possible. He practiced what he preached, and his mind and memory were as sharp in his nineties as they were in his younger years.

I sent him a card on his ninety-sixth birthday, and asked him how it felt to be ninety-six. I received a prompt, handwritten reply, which said:

> Dear Mort:
> It's not so bad to be ninety-six.
> But oh, to be seventy again!

FINAL THOUGHTS

If a new pill suddenly appeared that would enable you to increase dramatically your powers of attention, observation, retention, and recall, such a pill would no doubt be hailed as a miracle, and people would gladly pay any price for it.

If you think for a moment, you will realize that the memory techniques you have been learning and using in this book accomplish these very things. They literally and painlessly force you to focus your attention and observe and register information in such a way as to assure reliable retention and recall. If you can see the truth of this memory pill analogy, you will have a better and clearer view of the concept, use, and value of Memory Control techniques.

When all is said and done, one of the greatest benefits of memory training for anyone is simply *knowing* that you can actually remember anything that you want to remember. I have no doubt that such a personal asset can make a great and positive difference in your lifetime.

May all your memories be good ones.

Appendices

Appendix A:

Answers to Quizzes

POSSIBLE ANSWERS FOR QUIZ ON PAGE 92

Name	Name Cue
Ashkanazy	ash can with Nazis
Peilet	pilot
Gotteson	got a son
Klowden	cloudy
Meiners	miners
Wideikis	wid' a kiss
Busch	bush
Rupchik	rough chick
Wrigley	chewing gum
Hirschberg	Hershey-burger
Robin	red breasts
Witherspoon	withering spoon
Koronowski	coroner out skiing
Endicott	end of cot
Grieg	creek, Greek
Byrne	burn, burnt
Kuehl	mule, fuel, cool

Name	Name Cue
Laflin	laughin', left in
Ott	hot, otter, odd
La Banco	the bank

ANSWERS TO QUIZ ON PAGE 101

1. Mahler
2. Okimoto
3. Wideikis
4. Buckley
5. Siegel

6. Deiro
7. Charise
8. Nicholas
9. Collins
10. Peterson

Appendix B:

A Review of the System of Memory Control

Over the years I have developed two main ideas that have enabled me to perceive memory training from a different point of view. The first idea is a different concept of memory training itself; the second was the realization that something other than association is at work as the master principle of memory.

THE CONCEPT

There is something that has been overlooked in other books and courses devoted to the training of memory. It is the concept that clarifies and simplifies the process of memory training. It is the concept of control, *Memory Control.*

Regardless of some claims to the contrary, you cannot as yet improve your innate, inborn memory capacity; but you *can* improve the depth and quality of your mind's information processing through the deliberate direction of your *conscious mind.* This can result in vastly improved memory performance.

In contrast to your comparative lack of control over your subconscious mind, you have virtually complete control over your conscious mind. Your conscious mind is your working memory. In the same way that you can control your conscious mind, you can control your working memory. This is the basis of the concept of Memory Control.

THE MASTER PRINCIPLE

To date, all books and courses in memory training have considered association the master principle of memory. In my work with associative memory techniques over the years, it has become clear to me that, though association is indeed central to all memory, there is something else involved, something broader in scope than association alone, something much closer to the core of memory itself. This something is *meaning*.

The one thing that your mind remembers best, above all other things, is meaning. Without meaning, there can hardly *be* anything for your mind to remember. Meaning is the raw material of your mind and the very substance of your memory. In the last analysis, it is the presence of meaning that determines our ability to remember *anything*. For these reasons, Memory Control recognizes meaning as the master principle of memory.

Many memory books mention meaning, of course, and they cite it as an important principle along with association, organization, visualization, repetition, attention, and interest. Other than such equal billing, the true significance of meaning in memory is rarely noted. It is interesting that this point is missed, because all the other ingredients that *are* noted *are the very things that create meaning*, without which no remembering could take place!

The primary importance of meaning is a core concept of this book. Think of it in this way:

1. The master principle of memory is meaning.
2. The master principle of Memory Control is the *intensification* of meaning.

MENTAL INFORMATION PROCESSING

Good memory is a matter of good learning. Good learning is

possible only through your mind's ability to process its information effectively. Such effective processing is at the heart of Memory Control training. You should now be well aware that your memory process involves the three stages of registration, retention, and retrieval.

If there is failure at any one of these stages, a failure of memory performance will result. Because of this inescapable fact, the objective of the techniques of Memory Control is to strengthen each of these three stages so that they can effectively interact for reliable recall.

1.   Registration: In order for you to learn something in the first place, your attention is required. Also helpful at this stage are your intention to remember and your desire to remember. The acronym AID (*a*ttention, *i*nterest, and *d*esire) is thus a powerful, natural memory aid to keep in mind.

2.   Retention: To strengthen your retention, something more effective than simple repetition is needed. Memory Control uses various techniques of association, visualization, and organization, which provide the *meaning* that effectively reinforces retention.

3.   Retrieval: Even if you first pay attention to register new material, and then reinforce your retention with associative meaning, your memory may still fail in this third stage if there is no specific means of retrieval at hand.

Just as attention is required for registration, and associative meaning is required for retention, the main requirement for the third stage is a retrieval cue. To a large extent, all Memory Control procedures revolve around the recognition, creation, and control of retrieval cues.

THE RETRIEVAL CUE

A retrieval cue is anything that can trigger memory recall. Retrieval cues are limitless in number and kind. For instance, ordinary conversation is a continuous flow of retrieval cues; one idea leads to another.

How retrieval cues work is explained in detail in Chapter 3.

THE TECHNIQUES OF MEMORY CONTROL

Any device, technique, method, or strategy that creates or intensifies meaning is a technique of Memory Control. As a technique of Memory Control, association is especially important because all the techniques listed previously involve association to one degree or another. Keep in mind William James's observation that the mind is an associating machine. Remember that the more associations there are, the more meaning there is; and the more meaning, the better and more easily you will remember.

SUMMARY OF THE SYSTEM OF MEMORY CONTROL

1.   The key to greater memory performance is *control* of your mind's information processing stages: registration, retention, and retrieval.

2.   The master principle of memory is *meaning.*

3.   The master principle of Memory Control is the *intensification* of meaning.

4.   The basic unit of Memory Control is the *retrieval cue.*

5.   The retrieval cue techniques of association, mental imagery, and organization are used to enhance meaning. These control techniques produce effective information processing, resulting in *sound registration, prolonged retention,* and *reliable retrieval.*

Appendix C:

A Glossary of Terms and Techniques

For easy reference, the following are brief definitions of various terms and techniques used in this book. A more detailed treatment of each item plus in-depth examples can, of course, be found in the text itself.

ABC rhyme file: A mental filing system based on the twenty-six letters of the alphabet.

Accessibility: If a memory is accessible, it can be recalled. If it is available (stored in memory) but not accessible, it cannot be recalled unless the proper retrieval cue is used.

Acronym: A first-letter mnemonic in which each letter of a word has specific meaning. Example: HOMES is an acronym for the five Great Lakes (Huron, Ontario, Michigan, Erie, and Superior). Acronyms are miniature mental filing systems.

Acrostic: A succession of words in which the first letter of each has specific meaning. Example: *Every Good Boy Does Fine* (names of the five lines of the treble clef music staff).

AID: An acronym for *A*ttention, *I*nterest, and *D*esire.

Answering machine reminder: Reminder methods for remembering to turn on or turn off a telephone answering machine.

ARC: An acronym for *A*utomatic *R*epetition by *C*assette.

Association: The process by which ideas, thoughts, and facts are mentally connected.

Attention: The first requirement for good learning. Good learning results in good remembering.

Availability: The condition of being stored in memory, whether or not the information is accessible to recall.

Basic Unit of Memory Control: The retrieval-cue.

Belt reminder: A tightener type of external reminder using one's belt.

Blanks: People's names that seem meaningless in themselves. Examples: Grzynski, Lirgus, and Shantrell.

Body file: A mental filing system that uses places on the body or spaces around the body as file cues.

Brain Chain: A mental filing system without prearranged retrieval cues which associates successive items of information until a completed associative chain is formed.

CCR System: Letters stand for convert, connect, and review, a memory system for remembering names, faces, and facts about people. It is also the basis for this book's systems for remembering numbers, things filed mentally, English and foreign vocabulary, and other information.

Chunking: To "chunk" in memorizing numbers is to take two, three, four or more digits and combine them into one unit of meaning. Example: 637 can be one money-unit, or $6.37. Or, 10314112741, an eleven digit number, can be chunked into only 3 meaning units for easy memory as follows: Halloween, April Fool, and Pearl Harbor. (10/31, 4/1, and 12/7/41).

Coding: Coding is the application or intensification of meaning with names, numbers, or other items for easier memorization and recall. Such coding is what effects the transfer of the item to be remembered from short-term memory to long-term memory.

Concrete: Term used to denote mentally picturable names, ideas, or facts.

COPE: An acronym for *C*ome early, *O*ne at a time, *P*ace, and *E*arly review. It is used to retain control in meeting groups of people.

Conscious mind: Awareness, that part of your mind which is under your control. As such, it is your working memory.

Conversion: The conversion of a meaningless name, fact, or concept into a manageable unit of meaning, for easier association, visualization, or organization.

Cross-indexing: The process of providing your mind with multiple cues for easier recall of particular items of information later on.

Cue: You cue your memory with retrieval cues in order to trigger the process of remembering.

DART: Acronym for *D*irect *A*ccess *R*etrieval *T*echnique.

Displacement: Switching an item from one location to another to make the item an attention-compelling retrieval cue.

Diverse association: A term William James used (along with multiple association) as part of his statement that the best memory is the one that forms the most associations around a fact or idea, while weaving them into systematic relations with each other.

Ear reminders: A category of external reminders that can be heard.

External reminders: Reminders originating *outside* of your mind, as in contrast to Internal Reminders which originate within your mind. External Reminders are of the see, hear, or feel variety. The characteristics which determine their effectiveness are their degree of Activity, Specificity, Repeatability, and Timeliness.

Exaggeration: A technique used in mental picturing to create a more vivid impression.

Face cue: A facial feature which is selected for vivid mental connection with a person's name.

File place: This term is synonymous with File-Cue, File-Word, or File-Folder, in Mental Filing. Each such File-Place acts as a *direct access* retrieval-cue, recalling to mind whatever was deliberately and consciously associated with it previously.

Fingertip system: A simple technique using fingertips and spaces between the fingers to recall the number of days in any particular month.

First-Letter Mnemonic: An acronym, acrostic, or successive-syllable mnemomic.

FLO: An acronym reminder for *F*requency, whatever is *L*inked, and the *O*utstanding. These three characteristics are the things that memory remembers easiest, quickest, and best.

Floor reminder: A simple, commonsense external reminder that uses the floor as a retrieval cue.

House file: A mental filing system using a known sequence of items in your house or apartment as retrieval cues.

Image: As used in memory training, the image, imagery, or imaging is the imagined or visualized picture conjured up in your mind's eye. Imaging also includes your mind's ear and all of your other senses.

Impression: An impression (or registration) is the learning of something in the first place.

Industrial-strength reminders: External reminders of such a compelling nature that they are literally impossible to forget.

Inescapable reminders: External reminders that are so obvious or repetitious, usually due to their location, that there is no way to ignore them.

Information processing: The three-stage mental process through which incoming data is screened and processed: registration, retention, and retrieval.

Internal reminders: Reminders originating in your mind and triggering memory from within. In this book, all methods and techniques are internal reminders except those specifically labeled as external reminders which originate outside of the mind.

Link: Things that are linked together by association are the very things the mind remembers easiest and best. Link, linked, and linking describe the technique in action. To link is synonymous with *to associate* or *to connect*.

Loci: Latin for location or place. The method of loci is a classical technique in the art of memory, used over twenty-five hundred years ago by the ancient Greeks, Romans, and Hebrews. The house file and the body file are examples of this method of loci brought up to date.

Long-term memory (LTM): In contrast to short-term memory, LTM is what is usually meant when people speak of memory. Long-term memories reside in our unconscious minds. In this sense, LTM and the unconscious are synonymous. Memories retained and recalled over long periods of time belong to this category.

Memorization: The deliberate action of learning something. Memorization *is* learning. Memory Control provides easy and quick ways of committing things to memory, in contrast to tedious rote repetition.

Memory: Memory is the mind's ability to retain and revive past experience.

Memory aid: Anything that helps you remember.

Memory Control: Commonsense management of the three stages of your mind's information processing system of registration, retention, and retrieval.

Memory maintenance: The TRU formula for memory reinforcement—*T* for think about the information occasionally; *R* for repeat, review, or recite it; *U* for use the information in conversation or any other appropriate way. Any or all of these TRU components, or merely mentally recalling the information, will maintain its availability and accessibility to recall.

Memory training: Memory is a skill, trainable at will. By practicing and using the techniques of Memory Control, you will develop a trained and reliable memory for the things you want to remember.

Mental filing: Prearranged, organized sequences of retrieval cues work as a mental filing system when they are associated, visualized, and reviewed in connection with specific items of information to remember.

Mental imagery: See *Image*.

Mental holding device: Any First-Letter Mnemonic, mental filing system, or other memory aid that holds the information in memory for you so that you can reliably recall it.

MIETR principle: An acronym for the overall idea of mnemonics—*Make It Easier To Remember*.

Mnemonic: A mnemonic is simply *anything* that helps you remember better. Also called a mnemonic device or cue.

Multiple association: See *Diverse association*. Literally many associations of varying kinds.

Multisensory registration: Initial learning of a fact, name, number, idea, or other information through sight, sound, taste, touch, smell, and any and all other possible sensations.

Name conversion: See *Conversion*.

Name cue: In the CCR System for names and faces, a meaningless name is converted into a meaningful thought or picture symbol for easier association, visualization, or organization. Example: Okimoto becomes the name cue *locomotive*. Sam becomes the picturable name cue *Uncle Sam*.

Number-Meaning Method: This is really the CCR method as applied to the memorization and recall of numbers. Meaningless numbers are converted to meaningful thought or picture symbols in the form of sentence cueing, which is then easily decoded back into the original numbers.

Number-rhyme file: A mental filing system based on retrieval cues that rhyme with the numbers used.

One-trial learning: A term used in psychology to denote things that are remembered after only one exposure. These things are usually so outstanding or emphatic that they can hardly be forgotten once experienced.

Paired associates: Things you deliberately connect or associate in pairs. In Chapter 3 you mentally associated *meatball* with *envelope* and *Ivory Soap* with *screwdriver*. If you participated in this exercise properly, you had no difficulty whatsoever in recalling one of these words when its paired associate was given.

PAR Formula: As a formula for better remembering, PAR means *P*ay *A*ttention and
*R*emember—with *P*ositive *A*ction
*R*eminders—for *P*ower *A*ssisted
*R*ecall.

PAR techniques: The PAR techniques are *P*icture, *A*ssociate, and *R*eview, in mental filing.

Pattern recognition: Recognizing patterns is always a helpful memory aid, especially with numbers.

Pause method: A method used for recapturing a lost thread of thought or conversation.

Picture symbol: Something you can see in your mind's eye after converting it from something unpicturable or abstract in its original form.

Pocket or purse displacement reminder: See *Displacement.*

Positive action reminder: Any reminder that works easily, instantly, and reliably.

Five P's of preparation: *P*roper *P*reparation *P*revents *P*oor *P*erformance.

Principle of learning: Associating new facts or experiences with previous knowledge. Combining the new with the old completes the cycle of learning.

Reconstruction technique: Thinking back to reconstruct past and "forgotten" events, facts, or experiences.

Registration: Learning something in the first place. The first stage in the three stages of remembering.

Reinforcement: The strengthening of any or all of the three R stages of remembering.

Remembering to remember: The use of an appropriate external reminder to prompt recall of mentally filed material or any previously memorized information for specific action, use, or periodic review.

Reminder names: Names that have no specific meaning, but which can remind you of something. Examples: *Campbell* and *soup, Simmons* and *mattress.*

Reminder principle: One thing leads to another, and one

thing reminds you of another. Deliberate use of this phenomenon is the basis of Memory Control training.

Retention: The mind's ability to hold and store information, the second stage in the three Rs of remembering.

Retrieval: The process of calling up information from mental storage. Retrieval is the third stage in the three Rs of remembering.

Retrieval cue: The basic unit in Memory Control. *Anything* that can trigger memory recall is a retrieval cue—a word, a phrase, a sight, a sound, a touch, a taste, a smell, an emotion, or even a memory that itself triggers another memory in your mind.

Retrieval failure: What we speak of as forgetting is really a failure in the retrieval stage of memory. The "forgotten" item is still in storage, but we have not found the correct retrieval cue to get it back out. It is available but not accessible. It is like something on the tip of your tongue. You know it's there, but you can't bring it voluntarily to mind unless or until the right retrieval cue reminds you of it.

Ring reminder: An external reminder technique using a finger ring as a retrieval cue.

ROAM: An acronym reminder for *R*ecognize *O*r *A*dd *M*eaning.

Rote: A memorizing procedure usually resulting in mindless repetition. Since *meaning* is absent, the memory does not endure.

Rubber band reminder: An external reminder device with a rubber band.

SALT System: Acronym to remind you to *S*ay (and *S*pell) the name, *A*sk about it, *L*earn it, and *T*erminate the conversation using the name again.

Sentencing: Synonymous with sentence cue. With this procedure, you code meaning in sentence form, which, upon decoding, reproduces the original information.

Separate Syllable Technique: Separating the syllables in a name or word to make it more meaningful or picturable. Example: *Sampson* converts to *Sam and son. Monticello* becomes *Monti's cello,* or *mound o' Jell-O.*

Short-term memory (STM):   Synonymous with your conscious mind, your working memory.

Shoelace reminder: An external reminder of the tightener type.

Sight reminder: The category of reminders that you see.

Similar Sound: A conversion technique for learning names or new words. Examples: Silvestri = silver strings, Siegel = sea gull.

Sleeve reminder: An external reminder of the "tightening" type.

Split-brain theory: Refers to the two hemispheres of the brain. The left is involved with logic and straight thinking. The right hemisphere is involved with creativity, imagination, and intuition. Memory techniques primarily exercise the right side of the brain, developing the powers of imagination and creativity as well as memory.

SRS Formula: *S*imilar Sound, *R*hyme, *S*eparate Syllables. These are conversion techniques.

Starting Over Method: A means of overcoming momentary mental blanks, based on the theory of state-dependent recall, explained in Chapter 12.

Subconscious mind: The storehouse of long-term memory.

Tactile reminders: External reminders that you feel.

Talking Technique: An alternative method to mental picturing. Used in conjunction with picturing, memory and recall are strengthened.

Telephone reminder: An external reminder technique to remember to make previously promised phone calls.

Tie reminder: An external reminder of the tightener type, using a tie.

USA Formula: Formula for vivid mental picturing—The *U*nusual: *S*ee it in *A*ction.

Whatever Method: An approach to recalling lost thoughts.

Working concept: The working concept of this book is Memory Control.

Working memory: The constant interchange between your short-term memory and your long-term memory constitutes the continuous moment-by-moment, day-by-day functioning of your working memory.

Wristwatch alarm reminder: An external reminder you hear, using an alarm watch.

Wristwatch reminder: An easy and handy external reminder using a wristwatch.

Written reminder: Anything you write down as a reminder.

Appendix D:

Bibliography

Atkinson, Richard C., and Shiffrin, Richard M. "The Control of Short-Term Memory," *Scientific American* (August 1971).

Baddeley, Allen D. *The Psychology of Memory.* New York: Basic Books, 1976.

Bartlett, F. C. *Remembering.* Cambridge: University Press, 1932.

Bower, Gordon H. "Analysis of a Mnemonic Device," *American Scientist* 58 (1970).

Bower, Gordon H., ed. *Human Memory.* New York: Academic Press, 1977.

Bugelski, B. R. *Principles of Learning and Memory.* New York: Praeger Publishers, 1979.

Fincher, Jack. *Human Intelligence.* New York: Putnam, 1976.

Freese, Dr. Arthur S. *The End of Senility.* New York: Arbor House, 1978.

Furguson, Marilyn. *The Brain Revolution.* New York: Taplinger, 1973.

Gruneberg, Michael, and Morris, Peter. *Aspects of Memory.* London: Methuen Co., Ltd., 1978.

Gruneberg, M. M.; Morris, P. E.; and Sykes, R. N., eds. *Practical Aspects of Memory.* New York: Academic Press, 1978.

Halacy, D. S., Jr. *Man and Memory.* New York: Harper and Row, 1970.

Herold, Mort. *A Memory System That Works.* Cassette-Workbook Course. Hazel Crest, IL: Memory Improvement Services, 1980.

Hilgard, Atkinson, and Atkinson. *Introduction to Psychology.* New York: Harcourt Brace Jovanovich, 1979.

James, William. *Principles of Psychology,* Vol. 1. New York: Henry Holt & Co., 1890.

Katona, George. *Organizing and Memorizing.* New York: Columbia University Press, 1940.

Kihlstrom, John F. and Evans, Frederick J., eds. *Functional Disorders of Memory.* Hillsdale, NJ: Lawrence Erlbaum Associates, 1979.

Luria, A. R. *The Mind of a Mnemonist.* New York: Basic Books, 1968.

Norman, Donald A. *Memory and Attention.* New York: John Wiley and Sons, 1976.

Roth, David M. *Roth Memory Course.* Cleveland: Ralston Publishing Co., 1955 (1918).

Russell, Peter. *The Brain Book.* New York: Hawthorn, 1979.

Sommer, Robert. *The Mind's Eye.* New York: Dell, 1978.

Taylor, Gordon Rattray. *The Natural History of the Mind.* New York: E. P. Dutton, 1979.

Tulving, Endel. "Cue-Dependent Forgetting," *American Scientist* 62 (1974).

Yates, Frances A. *The Art of Memory.* Chicago: University of Chicago Press, 1966.